Expiatory temple of the Sagrada Familia

THE MASTERPIECE OF ANTONI GAUDÍ

EXPIATORY TEMPLE OF THE

Sagrada Familia

PHOTOGRAPHS
**CARLOS GIORDANO &
NICOLÁS PALMISANO**

MUNDO FLIP EDICIONES

CONTENTS

THE ORIGINS OF THE TEMPLE

THE TEMPLE OF THE PEOPLE

Nowadays, the Sagrada Familia is well-known throughout the world, but it actually started out as a local project, conceived and financed by a Christian association.

The emergence of the Sagrada Familia was fruit of a concrete social, political and cultural reality. In the last third of the 19th century, Catalan society kept an eye on what was changing in the world while at the same time was trying to recapture its identity as a people. This nationalist feeling was linked to a spiritual resurgence that spread through the lower to the upper classes; from the political class up to great figures in Catalan arts and literature. Within this con-text, Josep Maria Bocabella, President and Founder of the Association of Devotees to Saint Joseph, a religious group in Barcelona which by 1878 had already acquired 500,000 followers, decided to erect a temple funded by his own savings and donations from wor-shippers. Thus, the Sagrada Familia was born, a church made for and built by the people. On the 19th of March of 1882, its first stone was laid. In the Notarial Deed of the Ceremony its purpose was expressed: "Awake from tepid-ness those drowsy hearts. May Faith exult. Be charitable. Contribute so the Lord takes pity on the country..." What Bocabella couldn't imagine was to what extent this temple, which had been inspired by his faith in Saint Joseph, would eventually become one of the works of reference for architecture of all time. The shaper of this magnificent work was Antoni Gaudí, who would brilliantly transform this former neo-gothic style project into an absolutely unique temple.

THE ORIGINS OF THE TEMPLE
A glance at the events of the time

At the end of the 19th century Barcelona was a city in full industrialisation and enjoyed a rich cultural life. Its bourgeoisie promoted artistic projects of all kind, while religious spirit was gathering momentum. Within this context the temple of the Sagrada Familia was born: what started as the dream of Barcelonan, Josep Maria Bocabella, would in time become Gaudí's dream and the city's symbol.

The temple's promoter

The idea of erecting a temple in honour of the Holy Family came from Josep Maria Bocabella, a Barcelona bookseller. A learned man of strong religious conviction, Bocabella was President of the Association of Devotees to Saint Joseph.

In 1872, he travelled to Rome to offer to the Pope, on behalf of the association, a silver reproduction of a picture of Sagrada Familia. Before returning to Spain he passed through the Italian village of Loreto which is famous for its basilica and where, according to tradition, is the house where Joseph, Mary and Jesus lived. Bocabella was amazed by this church and decided to make a replica in Barcelona. However, he soon abandoned the idea and opted to build a new and original temple.

The House in Loreto. The Loreto basilica was where Bocabella took the decision to build a temple in Barcelona. Within its interior is the house where apparently Jesus, Mary and Joseph lived in Nazareth.

The promoter. Driven by his devotion to Saint Joseph, Bocabella wanted to dedicate a temple to the Holy Family.

CHRONOLOGY
KEY FACTS ABOUT GAUDÍ'S PERIOD

1853
Otis invents the lift
The inventor Elisha G. Otis presented the first lift with anti-fall safety device.

1865
Abolition of slavery in the USA
The end of the American Civil War meant freedom for the slaves.

1867
The first volume of the book *The Capital*
It was in this essay that Karl Marx dissected the capitalist system.

1870
The Third French Republic
King Louis Napoleon III abdicated after the defeat of France in the war against Prussia.

1874
Cezanne sells his first painting *Maison de Pendu.* The artist was ignored in his time and hardly ever publically exhibited his work.

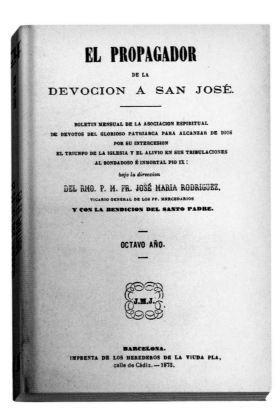

Bourgeoisie Splendour

Catalonia, with the city of Barcelona at its helm, was the region in Spain that most quickly adapted to the changes provoked by the Industrial Revolution. While the rest of Spain continued being basically agricultural, a solid industrial framework was being created in Catalonia. This economic prosperity led to a flourishing bourgeoisie that became promoter, as well as client or patron, of numerous artistic projects.

El Propagador
Was the Association of Devotees to Saint Joseph's magazine. It was in 1873 that the idea to build a temple was published for the first time.

DATA
TEXTILE INDUSTRY IN CATALONIA

The textile industry was pioneering in its use of steam machinery.

Textile mills:	Manual	Mechanical
1841	24.880	231
1850	24.008	5.580
1861	12.026	9.695

The spirit of the period

In the 19th century, Catalonia underwent an unprecedented cultural renewal, reflected by its literary, artistic and architectonic creations. This movement was known as the *Renaixença* (the Renaissance), owing to the fact that a genuine resurgence of cultural values was taking place at a time when the Catalan language's importance as first language was being recuperated.

Barcelona's coat of arms
The city's emblem was frequently used in the architecture of the period.

A new religious impetus

Josep Maria Bocabella's religious fervour wasn't an isolated case as towards the end of the 20th century Catalonia was experiencing a period of great spirituality, coinciding with the millennium celebration of the monastery of Montserrat (1880) and the proclamation of its Virgin as Patron Saint of Catalonia the following year.

1881
IS THE YEAR when the Virgin of the monastery of Montserrat is declared Patron Saint of Catalonia.

Montserrat monastery

1875
Alfonso XII King of Spain
Exiled from the age of 11, he recovered the throne for the Bourbons.

1879
Thomas Edison invents the electric bulb
This invention led to the generalization of electrical illumination.

1883
The Chicago School
After the city fire in 1871, construction commenced on numerous skyscrapers.

1887
The automobile is born
Karl Benz and Gottlieb Daimler boosted the automobile industry with the combustion motor.

THE LOCATION OF THE TEMPLE
Communion between architecture and urbanisation

Bocabella conceived the Sagrada Familia as an expiatory temple, in other words, financed by the alms of the faithful. He himself searched for donations in order to buy a centrally located plot of land in the Eixample, but his limited budget obliged him to look elsewhere. In 1881 the site of the future temple was paid for with the 172,000 pesetas (1.034 euros) he had accumulated under the floor tiles of his bookstore.

The city expands

The Sagrada Familia witnessed Barcelona's expansion. At the beginning of the 19th century, the city was experiencing an unprecedented demographic explosion. Growing industry was attracting thousands of workers to the city which, surrounded by an ancient defensive wall, was no longer able to hold all its inhabitants. Sanitary conditions were abysmal and in 1854 a cholera epidemic broke out practically decimating the population. The authorities believed it necessary to knock down the medieval wall and on the 24th of August of the same year, demolition work commenced and was to continue until 1856. From then on, Barcelona carried on expanding and underwent a period of great urban development, which ended up bestowing on the city its current appearance.

The turn of the 20th century. The Sagrada Familia can be seen in the distance, viewed from Hospital Sant Pau.

DATA
INHABITANTS OF BARCELONA

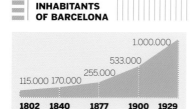

1.000.000
533.000
255.000
170.000
115.000

| 1802 | 1840 | 1877 | 1900 | 1929 |

Walled Barcelona
The walls that surrounded the city were constructed in the thirteenth century, during the reign of James I the Conqueror.

The temple of the Sagrada Familia
The temple is located on the right-hand side of the Barcelona Eixample, an area that was mainly taken up by factories in the 19th century.

CHRONOLOGY
KEY FACTS ABOUT GAUDÍ'S PERIOD

1888
Foundation of the UGT union
This trade union arose in Barcelona influenced by Marxist ideology.

1894
Invention of the radio. The Italian Guglielmo Marconi was the first person who managed to transmit radio signals.

1895
First cinema showing
Took place in Paris, organised by its inventors, brothers Auguste and Louis Lumiere.

1898
Independence of the Island of Cuba
After its defeat in the war against the United States, Spain lost the colony of Cuba.

1899
Foundation of F.C. Barcelona
A Swiss residing in Barcelona, Johan Camper was founder of the football club.

The Sagrada Familia temple

In 1928, the temple's surroundings were still in construction. When work began, this area of the Eixample, a little out of the way from the centre, was a neighbourhood inhabited by workers.

Cerdá, the creator of the Eixample
Architect and town planner, he encountered many obstacles at the start of the project, but little by little managed to convince the sceptics.

The Barcelona Eixample

Bocabella was convinced from the start that the Sagrada Familia had to be situated in the Eixample. This urban development project, devised by the engineer Ildefons Cerdá, was approved in 1859 and consisted of a great network of perpendicular and traversing streets. The blocks weren't squared but had bevelled edged corners (chamfers) which facilitated visibility. In each block, building on only two sides was permitted so that the rest could be dedicated to gardens. Cerdá also planned that the neighbourhood would possess communitary services such as a school, a civic centre and a market. All in all, it was a project for an egalitarian city designed to be enjoyed by its inhabitants.

The Eixample Project
Barcelona's magnificent urban expansion project contributed to the creation of a more egalitarian city. It was devised that every zone would have all the services that the citizen required.

1900
First zeppelin flight
The German Count Ferdinand von Zeppelin invented this aircraft lighter than air.

1900
Freud publishes *The Interpretation of Dreams*
This book sets out the basis for the theory of psychoanalysis.

1903
First piloted flight
The brothers Wilbur and Orville Wright invented the first aeroplane propelled by an engine.

1905
Einstein announces the theory of relativity
The German scientist revolutionized the classical concepts of physics.

THE FIRST STONE IS LAID

A temple is born with a neo-gothic stamp

The official date of birth of the temple of the Sagrada Familia is the 19th of March 1882, falling on the festival of Saint Joseph. The laying of the first stone was a great public event which was attended by all of Barcelona's civil and ecclesiastical authorities. This first stone was to serve as the base for the temple projected by Sagrada Familia's first architect, Francisco del Villar.

Francisco del Villar's project

When Bocabella ruled out the idea of reproducing the Loreto basilica, he entrusted the project to Francisco del Villar, a diocesan architect who in 1877 had offered his services free of charge to work on the plans for the new temple. Del Villar planned a neo-gothic church, the style in fashion for religious architecture and his project consisted of a church with three naves, a large-sized crypt and a high needle-shaped bell tower.

✳ Original drawing of the project by the architect Del Villar
Francisco del Villar planned a temple with elements typical of the neo-gothic period such as large honeycomb windows, exterior buttresses and a high needle shaped campanile.

CHRONOLOGY
KEY FACTS ABOUT GAUDÍ'S PERIOD

1908
Auguste Rodin sculpts *The Kiss*
This sculpture, along with *The Thinker*, is one of this French sculptor's most famous works.

1911
Amudsen arrives at the South Pole
The Norwegian explorer was the first man to reach the South Pole.

1914
First World War
Known as the Great War, it lasted until 1918 and involved 32 countries.

1916
Birth of Dadaism
This artistic movement emerged as a criticism of western culture.

1917
The Russian Revolution
After overthrowing the Tsar, Russia became a Soviet state. Lenin was its first president.

The façade
The most characteristic elements of the first façade planned for the temple are the bell tower, the large windows and the access stairs with their five entranceways.

Del Villar the architect
This diocesan architect devised the initial project and was at the helm of building work on the Sagrada Familia until his resignation in 1883.

1882
WAS THE YEAR
when the first stone was laid. After the ceremony, work was started on the construction of the crypt.

The first stone
The ceremony to mark the laying of the first stone was a great public event and had wide press coverage.

The ground plan. Del Villar planned a Latin cross layout measuring 97 metres long by 44 metres wide, with two lateral naves and a central one, as well as the transept and apse.

Del Villar's resignation
Del Villar's position in the project turned out to be ephemeral. Shortly after the supporting pillars of the crypt had been built, discrepancies commenced between Del Villar and Josep Maria Bocabella's technical assessor. Del Villar planned to build the columns with blocks cut from solid stone, while the management defended a much more economical system that consisted of erecting pillars with pieces of stone on the inside and outside which would later be filled in with masonry. The differences ended up being definitive and in 1883 Bocabella accepted Del Villar's resignation, fearful of remaining without funds to continue the project.

1918
End of the Great War
German surrender put an end to the war, in which almost 50 million people died.

1919
Gropius founds the Bauhaus
This German school of architecture and design was one of the most influential of modern art.

1922
Mussolini, head of government
After the so-called March on Rome, the Fascists take control in Italy.

1923
Dictatorship of Primo de Rivera
This military man headed the coup d'état and controlled Spain until 1930.

1926
Television is invented
The Scot John Logie Baird was the first person who managed to transmit moving images.

GAUDÍ TAKES OVER

The arrival of the young architect breathes new life into the temple

After Francisco del Villar's resignation, Josep Maria Bocabella offered control of the building work to his technical assessor, Joan Martorell, who declined but proposed one of his collaborators, Antoni Gaudí, to lead the project. It was the year 1883 and Gaudí was a young architect who by the age of 31 had already demonstrated excellent abilities. Gaudí's genius rapidly went beyond the original project, transforming it into a universal masterpiece.

Gaudí's first interventions

Enthused about the project, Antoni Gaudí officially became the temple's architect on the third of November, 1883. At that time, construction on the crypt's pillars, designed by Del Villar, had already begun and one of the first things that Gaudí did, was to transform them, providing them with naturalistic capitals. In 1884, the first plans of Sagrada Familia to be signed by Gaudí were for the design of the Chapel of Saint Joseph, situated in the temple crypt. Its construction was rapid and mass was first held at its altar on the 19th of March, 1885. Nonetheless, the crypt wasn't finished until 1891, with a few of the chapels still remaining to be decorated.

The architect in front of the temple
Gaudí showed how work progressed on the temple to numerous personalities of the period.

First steps
When Gaudí took over the project, the crypt was being built according to the former plan.

✳ Antoni Gaudí
When he took charge of the Sagrada Familia project in 1883, Gaudí was a young architect with little work constructed, but already well-known for his enormous energy and originality.

Gaudí's work-shop-study
Situated on the temple premises, it was where work on the plaster cast models and naves was carried out. Gaudí would improve on them replacing them as he went along.

31 YEARS OF AGE
was how old Gaudí was when he took on the project of the temple of the Sagrada Famlia.

The stamp of Gaudí

When Gaudí took on the temple project, he had only projected two important works: Vincens House and the lamp posts in Plaza Reial and Pla del Palau in Barceloneta. Despite his little experience and youth the architect designed an initial plan of the Sagrada Familia which he was never to abandon, carrying out some modifications which sought to improve on Del Villar's project. Nonetheless, he couldn't implement all the changes he would have liked given that he was restricted by the crypt's base, which had been built by the former architect. One of the ideas he had to do away with consisted in erecting the temple in diagonal direction, to fully orientate the Nativity façade towards the sunrise, and the Passion, towards the sunset.

The work table
The latter years of Gaudí's life were totally dedicated to the Sagrada Familia. His work table was in the temple's workshop-study.

Gaudí's room
In 1925, he moved into his workshop-study in Sagrada Familia. In a corner, near to his work table is the bed in which he slept.

1852
Gaudí is born in Reus, province of Tarragona.

1868
He moves to Barcelona to study architecture.

1875
Does military service in the Armed Infantry of Barcelona.

1876
His mother dies.

1878
He finishes architectural studies. He designs the lamp posts for Plaza Reial and the Pla del Palau commissioned by the City Council. He meets Eusebi Güell who becomes his friend and patron. He exhibits in the Universal Exhibition held in Paris in 1878.

1883
Commences work on The Caprice, in Comillas and the Vincens House in Barcelona. He leads the building project of the Sagrada Familia.

1886
Starts on the construction of Güell Palace.

1892
He travels to Tangiers to work on the project of the Franciscan missions in Africa.

1900
The Calvet House, is awarded the prize for best building by the City Council. Work commences on Park Güell.

1904
He receives the commission to remodel the Casa Batlló.

1905
Pere Milà entrusts him with the construction of his home: La Pedrera.

1906
He moves to a house in Park Güell with his father and niece. Months after, his father dies at the age of 93.

1909
Constructs the Sagrada Familia's schoolrooms, which were used up until the mid 1980's.

1910
He takes on the commission of a hotel project in New York.

1911
Ill with fever in Malta and then moves to Puigcerdà, where he draws up his will.

1912
His niece dies.

1914
Construction work on Park Güell is held up.

1918
His great friend and patron Eusebi Güell dies.

1925
He moves into the temple workshop in the Sagrada Familia.

1926
On the 7th of July he is knocked down by a tram. Three days later, he dies in the Santa Cruz hospital, aged 74.

GAUDÍ'S WORKS

Universal and innovative, Gaudí left an architectural legacy which continues to captivate for the originality of its technical and aesthetic resources.

01. Casa Calvet
City Council awards prize for best building of 1900.

02. Casa Batlló
Over the polychromatic façade the balconies appear to hang like bird nests.

03. Casa Vicens
Built between 1883 and 1888, it was Gaudí's first important project.

04. Finca Güell
It was his first commission by Eusebi Güell.

05. The Teresian College
Worked on the college situated in Barcelona.

06. Bellesguard
With this work, Gaudí commemorates Catalonia's past.

07. Güell Palace
Its austere façade contrasts with the exuberant design of its interior.

08. La Pedrera
One of Gaudí's masterpieces, which stands out for its sinuous façade and its rooftop chimneys.

09. The Caprice
Gaudí blended the Medieval style with the exuberance of oriental palaces.

10. Park Güell
Conceived as a project for a city garden, architectonic elements and nature are integrated into the landscape.

02

GAUDÍ'S PROJECT

IN SEARCH OF THE PERFECT TEMPLE

Antoni Gaudí wanted that mysticism and architecture blend into one in the Sagrada Familia, transforming each corner of the temple into a symbol of the Faith.

In the commission of the temple of the Sagrada Familia, Antoni Gaudí took the opportunity to explore all of its architectonic potential and to achieve what no other architect had managed for centuries before him: the construction of the perfect temple. With this goal in mind, he concentrated all his efforts on ensuring that the whole of the temple would be in perfect consonance with his final mission, which was none other than the celebration of liturgical rites. He therefore drew on all of his innovative artistic and architectonic resources so that they could be perfectly adapted to the practice of religious cult. With the passing of the years and propelled by his anxiety for perfection, Gaudí gathered a sound religious knowledge along with a growing faith, converting him into an expert on liturgical themes. The architect envisaged the Sagrada Familia as a Bible made of stone, which told the history and mysteries of the Christian faith. On the exterior of the temple he represented the Church by means of apostles, evangelists, the Virgin and the saints. The cross, which tops the main tower, symbolizes the triumph of Jesus' church and the façades evoke three transcendental moments in Christ's lifetime: his birth (Nativity), death (Passion) and resurrection (Glory). The interior refers to the universal church and the crossing, to the Celestial Jerusalem, mystic symbol of peace. All in all, Gaudí managed to combine his faith and his artistic genius to transform the Sagrada Familia temple into a universal masterpiece.

THE TEMPLE OF GAUDÍ

A unique project. With Gaudí in charge of the construction work, Sagrada Familia was acquiring greater significance, as much for its revolutionary structure as its complex symbolism.

Location and surroundings

Gaudí wanted the temple of the Sagrada Familia to become a focal point. He therefore devised an urban development plan which consisted of an eight-pointed star-shaped square. This design enabled the viewer to observe from his angle of vision, the central cimborio, measuring 170 metres high, and two façades at the same time. Due to the elevated cost of the land on which to build the square, Gaudí had to opt for a more restricted layout which consisted of a four-pointed star.

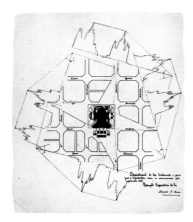

Gaudí's second urban development plan
Taken into account was how the temple would be seen by passers-by. The four-pointed star-shaped square meant the temple's silhouette could be seen from all angles.

> Everyone finds his things in the temple. The peasants see the hens, the scientists the zodiac signs, the theologians the genealogy of Jesus..."
>
> Antoni Gaudí

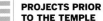
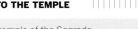

PROCESS
PROJECTS PRIOR TO THE TEMPLE

The temple of the Sagrada Familia was preceded by two other projects by Antoni Gaudí.

1892
The Tangier Missions
In this project, which was never built, the shape of the towers already stand out.

1898
The Güell Colony Crypt
In its church, Gaudí experimented with roofs, vaults and columns.

1902
Temple of the Sagrada Familia
Is the compendium of the experiments and innovations of earlier projects.

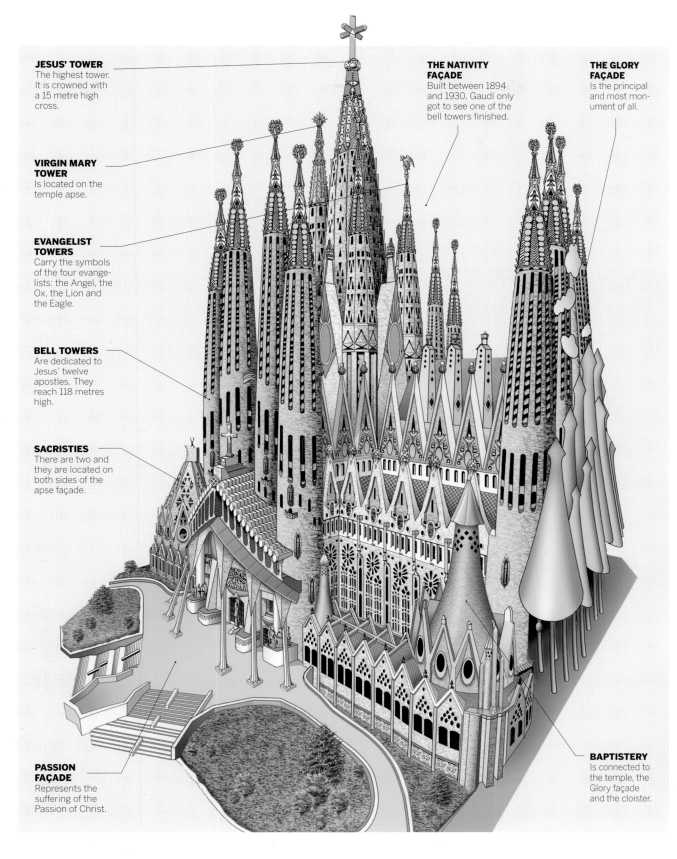

JESUS' TOWER
The highest tower. It is crowned with a 15 metre high cross.

VIRGIN MARY TOWER
Is located on the temple apse.

EVANGELIST TOWERS
Carry the symbols of the four evangelists: the Angel, the Ox, the Lion and the Eagle.

BELL TOWERS
Are dedicated to Jesus' twelve apostles. They reach 118 metres high.

SACRISTIES
There are two and they are located on both sides of the apse façade.

PASSION FAÇADE
Represents the suffering of the Passion of Christ.

THE NATIVITY FAÇADE
Built between 1894 and 1930, Gaudí only got to see one of the bell towers finished.

THE GLORY FAÇADE
Is the principal and most monument of all.

BAPTISTERY
Is connected to the temple, the Glory façade and the cloister.

The sketches and models

Following the project's general concept, Gaudí made plans of the temple working on large sections. To resolve the technical problems which would occur, he used models, plans and drawings which he kept in his workshop. Unfortunately, during the uprising of 1936 the plans were burnt, but plaster models were preserved and restored after the Spanish Civil War.

Study of monument, 1902
To evaluate the aesthetic effect of shapes and volume, Gaudí used drawings.

The Passion façade, 1911
Antoni Gaudí used drawings and models to design the façades.

Models. In order that Gaudí's projects could be visualized better, models of the temple were created on a scale of 1:10 and 1:25.

A MONUMENTAL WORK

Closer to God. The solemnity of the temple planned by Gaudí required enormous dimensions. Its numerous pinnacles and towers were nearer to heaven than any other building in the city.

The ground plan

The temple of the Sagrada Familia is a building in the form of a Latin cross, measuring 94 metres long by 60 wide. The main nave is made up of 5 naves: a central one which is 15 metres wide and 45 metres high, and two lateral ones on both sides. The arms of the cross correspond with two façades on the exterior: that of the Nativity and the Passion. There is a third façade, the Glory, situated at the start of the main nave. The apse, of lobular shape, is comprised of 7 chapels; below which a crypt is found.

The Nativity façade
According to Gaudí's project, in order that the temple could be viewed easily, it had to be surrounded by garden and park areas.

Pinnacles
The towers are topped by pinnacles which are decorated with lively and bright polychromatic mosaics.

The apse. It was finished in 1893, after three years of work.

14.000
PEOPLE
is the total capacity which the temple interior will hold when liturgy is held.

4.500
SQUARE METRES
is the surface area taken up by the premises of the Sagrada Familia.

7
DOORS
take up the main entrance of the temple, situated on the Glory façade, on Mallorca Street.

6
TOWERS
In pyramid arrangement, they articulate the crowning of the temple. Four towers are dedicated to the evangelists, one to Jesus and the other to the Virgin Mary.

ASSUMPTION CHAPEL
It is devoted to the Assumption of the Virgin and it can be directly accessed from the exterior.

Antoni Gaudí

The Temple is the construction par excellence and after that, only the house is"

The dimensions of the temple
Once finished, the temple will be 80 metres wide, 110 m long and 170 m high.

ANGLE OF VISION

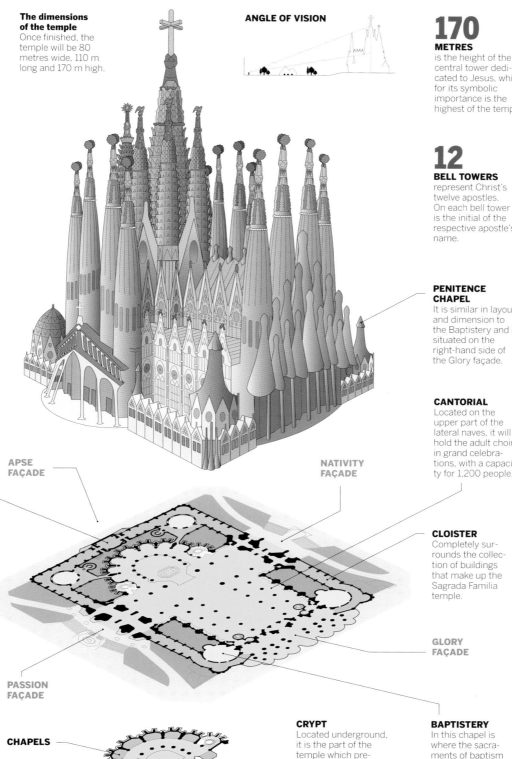

APSE FAÇADE

NATIVITY FAÇADE

PASSION FAÇADE

CHAPELS

STAIR

MAIN ALTAR

CRYPT
Located underground, it is the part of the temple which preserves more neo-gothic elements. At present it is the neighbourhood parish church.

170
METRES
is the height of the central tower dedicated to Jesus, which for its symbolic importance is the highest of the temple.

12
BELL TOWERS
represent Christ's twelve apostles. On each bell tower is the initial of the respective apostle's name.

PENITENCE CHAPEL
It is similar in layout and dimension to the Baptistery and is situated on the right-hand side of the Glory façade.

CANTORIAL
Located on the upper part of the lateral naves, it will hold the adult choir in grand celebrations, with a capacity for 1,200 people.

CLOISTER
Completely surrounds the collection of buildings that make up the Sagrada Familia temple.

GLORY FAÇADE

BAPTISTERY
In this chapel is where the sacraments of baptism will be administered.

The height of the temple
With Sagrada Familia, Gaudí recovered the vertical anxiety that the churches of the Middle Ages had pursued. These constructions towered over the civil buildings, which bestowed them with even more majesty and mysticism. Following this idea, Gaudí gave great ponderability to height in respect to the rest of the dimensions. The highest tower was dedicated to Jesus and reached 170 metres which meant that Gaudí could ensure visibility of his work from any viewpoint in the city.

COMPARISON
DIMENSIONS OF THE TEMPLE

The monument of the Sagrada Familia takes up an area similar to that of a large-sized football pitch (120x90 metres).

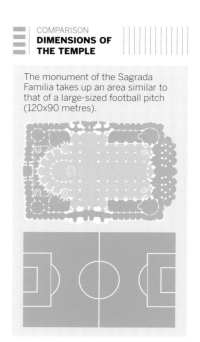

THE STRUCTURE

The global project. In the Sagrada Familia, Gaudí reunited and perfected the innovations and discoveries of his career as architect. For its structural conception, the temple represents the technical and artistic climax of its creator.

Revolutionary solution

Before Antoni Gaudí, Gothic architecture was the style which allowed the obtainment of great height with lighter support elements, but still required buttresses to sustain the structure from the outside. Gaudí wanted to dispense with buttresses and set about searching for technical solutions that former styles hadn't found. Finally, he devised a new method. It consisted of studying the weights of the building so that the constructive elements were those that would be adapted to bear the load. From there evolved the curious shapes which the temple of the Sagrada Familia took on, with leaning columns and hyperboloid vaults.

DATA
MEASUREMENTS OF THE TEMPLE INTERIOR

Width of naves	45 metres
Height of central nave	45 metres
Width of central nave	15 metres
Height of lateral nave	30 metres
Width of lateral nave	7,5 metres
Length of naves	90 metres
Between columns	7,5 metres
Width of transept	30 metres
Cross vault height	60 metres

Funicular
By putting weights along the string, Gaudí's funicular arches were obtained.

The inspiration
Trees inspire the columns used by Gaudí. They slightly lean and branch out in the upper part to support the vaults.

Stone columns
In each column, Gaudí used a different type of stone in relation to the weight it supported.

200 ton.
Montjüic stone

1.000 ton.
Granite stone

3.000 ton.
Basalt stone

6.000 ton.
Porfid stone

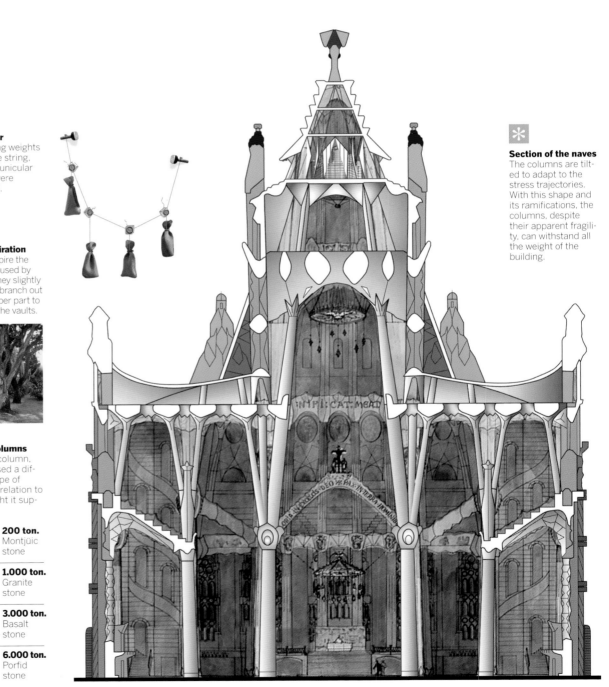

Section of the naves
The columns are tilted to adapt to the stress trajectories. With this shape and its ramifications, the columns, despite their apparent fragility, can withstand all the weight of the building.

The proportion of the temple

Gaudí set out the temple under a general proportion, which is repeated throughout each part of the building. These proportions are based on one unit, half and thirds. For example, the interior of the temple measures 90 metres long (unit), 60 metres wide (two-thirds) on the transept and 45 metres wide (half) in the naves.

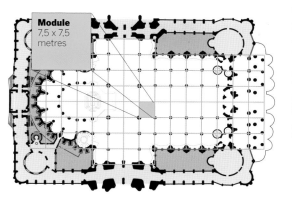

Module
7,5 x 7,5
metres

The modulation of the temple

The modulation is the basis on which the temple is based and is used to establish the different proportions of the ground plan and the layout of the different elements which make it up.

Funicular model of the church of the Güell Colony

Before applying the catenary arch in the Sagrada Familia, Gaudí developed this method in the Güell Colony.

✳ Columns and joints

For the development of the temple structure and its complex geometric shapes, Gaudí carried out various study models on the scale of 1:10. This one was done between 1918 and 1920.

Calculation of the structure

First of all, Gaudí calculated the weight of the elements of the building. Later he built a model with strings, from which he hanged weighted bags to simulate the shape of the inverted building. The strings formed arches, called funiculars, which followed the strength lines of the structure. After, he would photograph them and turning the images around he would obtain the structure.

COMPARISON
NEW ARCH CREATED BY GAUDÍ

Romanesque arch

Withstands great loads but requires buttresses and thick walls to avoid collapse. For this reason only small windows are permitted.

Gothic arch

Allows great height and large windows for the entry of light, but still needs exterior buttresses so that the building doesn't collapse.

Gaudí's arch

The catenary arch or funicular allows the obtainment of great height and large windows without the need for buttresses, given that due to its shape it distributes the weight itself.

01
The Passion façade (1972)
The towers rise 55 metres high and the columns and portico archways are being completed.

02
Antoni Gaudí
The architect with members of The Regionalist League.

03
The Nativity façade (1899)
A man contemplates the state of the work seven years after it began.

04
Central portal of the Passion façade (1965)
The façade reaches 11 metres high.

05
Collocation of the Annunciation group
Temple workers position the sculptures on the Nativity façade.

06
Views of the interior
View from the interior area of the temple during work on the Passion façade.

07
Rosary Chapel
Close-up of roof and cupola.

08
The apse
The apse exterior completed in 1893.

03

THE TEMPLE CRYPT

THE ENTRAILS OF THE TEMPLE

Gaudí managed to put his own mark on the crypt, despite not carrying out great modifications on the neo-gothic project planned by Francisco del Villar.

Excavation work on the crypt commenced between April and May in 1882, when the temple was still under the control of the diocesan architect Francisco del Villar. A few months later Del Villar resigned and Gaudí took over the project. However, the architect from Reus had to accept what had already been built, given that to drastically change the original plan would have supposed investing a large sum of money, which was completely out of the question considering that the temple was funded with the worshippers' alms. Even so, Gaudí managed to introduce some changes into the crypt which were more in keeping with his own architectural vision. Amongst his contributions stand out the construction of the ditch and the raising of the columns. Likewise, he decided to decorate the column capitals with naturalistic motifs, which the sculptor Llorenç Matamala was commissioned to work on. Located below the apse, the crypt is made up of seven apse chapels, in front of which are five others in a straight line, a deambulatory and a central area of almost circular shape measuring 40 metres long by 30 metres wide, over which the church presbytery will be situated. To reach this area two winding staircases were built and are situated on either side of the apse. These two stairs uniting the temple in vertical form, permit the accessibility between different levels and upper areas. Declared to be a World Heritage Site by UNESCO in the year 2005, the temple crypt has been used as a parish church since 1930.

THE TEMPLE CRYPT
The first part of the temple that was built

The crypt is situated below the apse, between the Nativity and Passion façades. It was the first part of the temple that they started work on, when the project was still led by architect Francisco del Villar. A year after construction work had commenced, he resigned from his post. Antoni Gaudí took on the position and soon put his unmistakeable stamp of genius on to the neo-gothic crypt.

The revision of the neo-gothic style

The crypt, which in Greek means hidden place, is a temple space which brings to mind the catacombs or subterranean places where the first Christians hid in times of persecution.

Gaudí took control of the construction of the temple when the raising of the crypt's columns had already commenced. The former project led by Del Villar was of pure neo-gothic style and Gaudí could only vary the elements which wouldn't affect the structure too much, such as raising the vault and adorning the capitals with naturalist details. He also surrounded the crypt with a deep ditch to prevent damp and, at the same time, to obtain illumination and direct and natural ventilation.

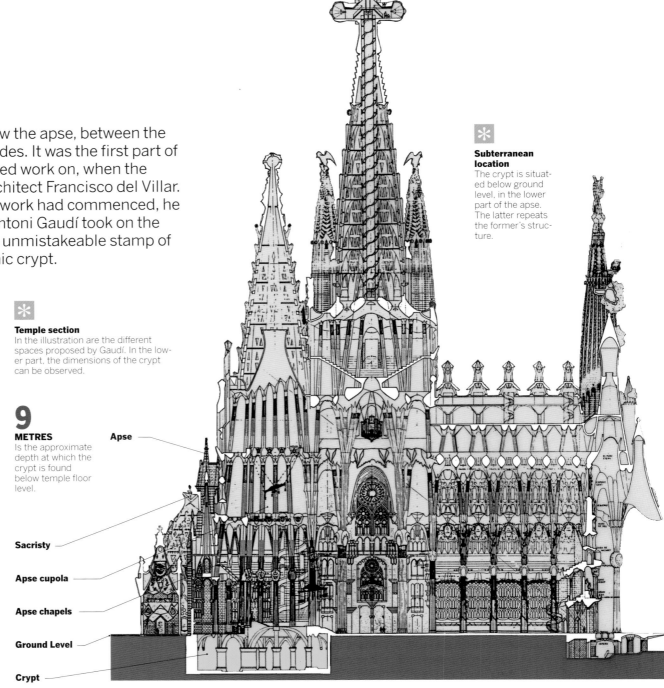

※

Subterranean location
The crypt is situated below ground level, in the lower part of the apse. The latter repeats the former's structure.

※

Temple section
In the illustration are the different spaces proposed by Gaudí. In the lower part, the dimensions of the crypt can be observed.

9
METRES
Is the approximate depth at which the crypt is found below temple floor level.

Apse

Sacristy

Apse cupola

Apse chapels

Ground Level

Crypt

3.619
DAYS OF WORK
Was the length of time required to build the crypt. It commenced on the 19th of March, 1882 and was finished 10 years later, in 1891.

The interior composition

The crypt is made up of seven chapels dedicated to the Holy Family of Jesus Christ which form a rotunda, in front of which are five other chapels in a straight line. Of these five chapels, the middle one houses the central altar, which is where mass is celebrated. According to what was originally planned, this central zone of the crypt will contain a reproduction of The Holy House of Nazareth, like the one venerated in Loreto.

Altar of The Holy House in Loreto

Candelabra
Gaudí designed the temple's liturgical objects.

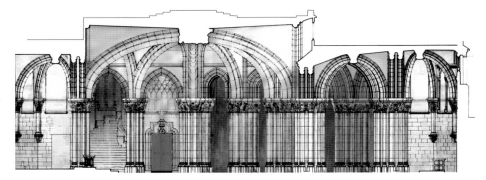

Section of the crypt
The central space is higher than the chapels. Thanks to this difference in height, Gaudí could open windows and naturally ventilate and illuminate the area.

1882
Construction commenced
The laying of the first stone was on the 19th of March. The same year excavation was completed.

1885
Work advances
The altar to Saint Joseph is finished, where mass is held despite the crypt being unfinished.

1936
Disasters of the Civil War
The three chapels that had been completely decorated were destroyed during the uprising of 1936.

THE ALTAR AND THE CHAPELS

Of neo-gothic style, the subterranean floor of the crypt, in which lie the remains of Antoni Gaudí and the temple's promoter Josep Maria Bocabella, has a central altar, twelve chapels and a wide deambulatory.

The apse chapels

The seven chapels which make up the semi-circle are dedicated to the Holy Family of Jesus. In the centre are the chapel of Saint Joseph, the Sacred Heart that represents Jesus' most human side, and that of the Immaculate Conception, dedicated to the Virgin Mary. Two other chapels are devoted to the Virgin's parents: Saint Joachim and Saint Anne. At one end, is the chapel of Saint John, Jesus' cousin, who was given the charge, at the Crucifixion, of looking after the Virgin Mary. At the opposite far end, is the chapel dedicated to Saint Elisabeth, Mary's cousin and Saint John's mother, and to her spouse Saint Zachariah.

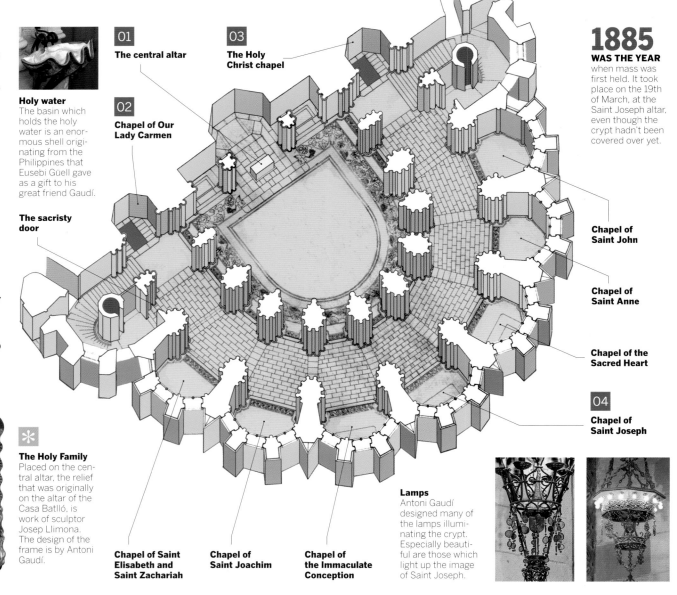

Holy water
The basin which holds the holy water is an enormous shell originating from the Philippines that Eusebi Güell gave as a gift to his great friend Gaudí.

01
The central altar

02
Chapel of Our Lady Carmen

03
The Holy Christ chapel

The sacristy door

1885
WAS THE YEAR when mass was first held. It took place on the 19th of March, at the Saint Joseph altar, even though the crypt hadn't been covered over yet.

Chapel of Saint John

Chapel of Saint Anne

Chapel of the Sacred Heart

04
Chapel of Saint Joseph

The Holy Family
Placed on the central altar, the relief that was originally on the altar of the Casa Batlló, is work of sculptor Josep Llimona. The design of the frame is by Antoni Gaudí.

Chapel of Saint Elisabeth and Saint Zachariah

Chapel of Saint Joachim

Chapel of the Immaculate Conception

Lamps
Antoni Gaudí designed many of the lamps illuminating the crypt. Especially beautiful are those which light up the image of Saint Joseph.

01

The central altar
Flanked by two chapels on each side, the central chapel holds the altar where mass is held at present. Presiding over it is an enormous relief representing the Holy Family.

02

Chapel of Our Lady Carmen
Gaudí wanted to be buried at the feet of this Virgin, to whom he was very devoted. His tombstone reads: *Antonius Gaudí Cornet, reusensis.*

03

The Holy Christ chapel
Is where Josep Maria Bocabella, founder of the temple, is buried.

04

Chapel of Saint Joseph
It was the first one built, owing to the great devotion that Josep Maria Bocabella felt for Saint Joseph.

05

The sacristy door
Is carved in wood with metal ornaments.

THE VAULTS

To improve its illumination and bestow it with new special aesthetic effects, Gaudí introduced some changes into the crypt vault system. As decoration, he placed a sculpted keystone in the centre of each one of the vaults.

The vault system

The crypt is covered over by a series of vaults supported by numerous Gothic style arches and columns. Each vault has a keystone or central stone on which different elements are sculpted. Gaudí modified Villar's project in order that the central vault, finished off with a great keystone representing the Annunciation, would be higher than the chapels. With this difference in height, he managed to add some small windows which gave better illumination and ventilation to the central nave.

Polychromatism
The keystone of the central vault is polychromatic and different golden shades were chosen to accentuate volume.

Windows
Gaudí made the central vault higher than the others. By doing this, enough space was generated to place various windows.

01

The central vault keystone
This polychromatic relief, a representation of the Annunciation by sculptor Flotats, positioned by Gaudí at the point where the two large arches converge.

Mary
Kneeling down with crossed arms, demonstrates her submission and loyalty. Mary accepts the complex mission which God has in store for her.

The Holy Spirit
Embodied as a dove, the Holy Spirit is in charge of carrying out the mission of the conception so that the son of God is born unto Mary.

The Archangel Gabriel
The archangel acts as God's messenger and with decisive attitude, announces to Mary that she has been the chosen one to conceive Jesus.

The keystone

It is an architectonic element that permits the finalizing of the nerves (continuations of the columns) in the highest part of a vault or in the middle of an arch. In the case of the crypt of the Sagrada Familia temple, these keystones are circular relieves of high artistic value.

10 PILLARS

are those which support the central nave. They are formed by bunches of columns.

22 KEYSTONES

are found on the crypt vaults. Each one of them shows different images and symbols.

The vault keystones

The crypt vaults are laid out in semi-circular shape surrounding the great vault of the central nave. In total, there are twenty-two. In the deambulatory, placed between the central nave and the apse chapels, we find eleven independent vaults, each of which are topped off with circular keystones containing different motifs of winged angels.

Also, the central altar and the nine chapels are covered by ten other vaults decorated with circular polychromatic keystones, on which the monograms of each one of the chapels are represented.

Plan of the crypt vaults

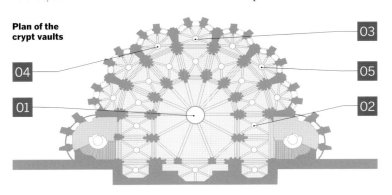

04
03
05
01
02

02 Keystone of wandering
An angel appears to emerge from the stone.

03 Keystone of the chapel of Saint Joseph
Represents Joseph's anagram.

04 Keystone of the chapel of the Immaculate Conception
It is Mary's anagram.

05 Keystone of the chapel of Saint Anne
An anagram carved in stone.

01

Capital with vegetation details
The leaves and other vegetation which cover the capitals were introduced by Gaudí in order to break with the strict neo-gothism of the crypt.

02

A detail from the Holy Christ chapel
Stars in polychromatic mosaic.

03

The Sacristy Door
Close-up of metal ornamentation.

04

Chapel of the Immaculate Conception
Sculpture of the Virgin of the chapel.

05

Floor detail
Polychromatic mosaic depicting a bird feeding on a vine.

06

Close-up of a window
Image of an angel with trumpet announcing the Final Judgement.

07

Angel on a column
Forms part of a group of two, four or six-winged angels, inspired by the book of the Apocalypse.

THE MONUMENT DEDICATED TO MARY

In consonance with his era, Antoni Gaudí was greatly devoted to the Virgin Mary and for this reason he dedicated the apse tower and the chapel of the Assumption to her.

The series of constructions which make up the apse façade are comprised of four architectonic elements: the mentioned apse which rises up as a majestic backdrop, the chapel of the Assumption, the two sacristies located on the sides and the cloister, which unites the chapel with the sacristies. The cloister is included as one of the many innovations introduced by Gaudí into the Sagrada Familia with regards to traditional churches, given that instead of being set on one side it works as an

element which unifies the numerous constructions which make up the Sagrada Familia monument. Where the cloister intersects with each façade there is a door dedicated to the Virgin. To show his successors how these doors should be decorated, Gaudí built the door dedicated to the Virgin of the Rosary, which he magnificently adorned with roses carved in stone, accompanied by sculptures and reliefs. The cult to the Virgin, was instituted as dogma by the Catholic Church from the time of Concilio de Trento

(1545-1563) and reached its maximum splendour in the 19th century. Marian fervour echoed throughout the field of the arts, as many artists were dedicating their work to the veneration of the Virgin Mary. Antoni Gaudí was also greatly devoted to the Virgin, as demonstrated by his wish to be buried in the chapel dedicated to the Virgin Carmen, which is situated in the temple crypt. For this reason, he believed it was essential to devote a significant part of the temple to the maternal figure of the Holy Family.

THE APSE
The perfecting of the Gothic

Constructed straight after the completion of the crypt, the apse of the Sagrada Familia temple is clearly Gothic inspired. Nonetheless, Antoni Gaudí's unique stamp is also apparent, who approached this architecture as "perfecting on the Gothic style".

The temple grows

Once the crypt was finished, work commenced on the apse, whose position over the former meant it repeated its structure. Gaudí, a fervent devotee to the Virgin, wanted to dedicate the apse to Mary. All the symbols and images adorning it are based on liturgical verses in allegiance to the Virgin, and the cimborio, which rises over the apse, is crowned by a large star, the *Stella matutina*, a classic Marian symbol. However, in the interior, the seven apse chapels commemorate the seven pains and pleasures of Saint Joseph, according to the wishes of its founder Bocabella, whose devotion to Saint Joseph gave rise to the temple.

Saint Clare
On the apse there are sculptures dedicated to the founders of religious orders like Saint Clare.

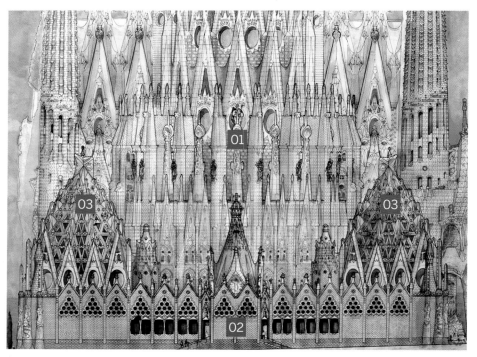

Apse façade. The drawing is an interpretation by Berenguer. **1.** Apse. **2.** Chapel of the Assumption. **3.** Sacristies.

1891
Just after finishing the crypt, Gaudí started work on the apse.

1892
After one year the exterior apse walls had been erected.

1893
Construction is completed on the apse exterior, after the third year.

Jesus' anagram
The letters *alfa* and *omega* recall that Jesus is the Beginning and the End.

Jesus' anagram
Jesus' initial is surrounded by a crown of thorns, which is a symbol of his martyrdom.

The Virgin's anagram
The crown situated over Mary's initial symbolizes her position as Queen of Heaven and Earth.

Saint Joseph's anagram
Joseph's initial is accompanied by narcissi, flowers which represent the purity and chastity of the saint.

Antoni Gaudí

The projecting elements must be combined with the recesses, in such a way that each convex element, which is placed in full light, puts the other in shadow"

THE NATURE OF STONE

The apse exterior is a reflection of the great fascination that Antoni Gaudí held for nature. Apart from their decorative role, the architect used vegetables and animals as mystic symbols.

The naturalistic vision of Antoni Gaudí

Gaudí was a great observer of nature. He had a deep admiration for all living beings and, in particular, plants and trees, which on numerous occasions were a source of inspiration in the aesthetic as well as technical sense. On one occasion he went so far as to say that his master was a tree which was growing near his workshop. Representations from the vegetable kingdom are frequent in his work, like the ears of wheat and floral motifs which top the pinnacles of the apse walls.

Wheat ear
Gaudí chose wheat as a Eucharist symbol and for being a high quality Mediterranean cereal.

Palm leaves
The upper part of the apse is decorated with palm leaves, cypress, olive, cedar, balsam fir and cinnamon, carved in stone.

Wild herbs
The humble herbs growing on the temple grounds were depicted on the apse pinnacles.

Dimensions
Gaudí calculated the dimensions of each element in order that they could be recognized a long distance away.

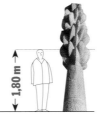

1,80 m

" It isn't possible to go ahead without leaning on the past and taking advantage of the effort and achievements of the generations that precede us"

Antoni Gaudí

Apse gargoyle. A wall lizard runs down the apse, as it is not allowed to enter the temple of the Sagrada Familia.

The gargoyles
These architectonic elements were first used in the Gothic period and were used to drain away rainwater accumulated on cathedral roofs.

The animals

In the Gothic period, cathedral gargoyles were fantastical and demonic beings. Gaudí preferred to use, for the Sagrada Familia apse, common animals traditionally associated with evil. The amphibians and reptiles on the walls are not allowed to enter the temple. All are head down, fleeing from the purity radiating from Mary's symbols.

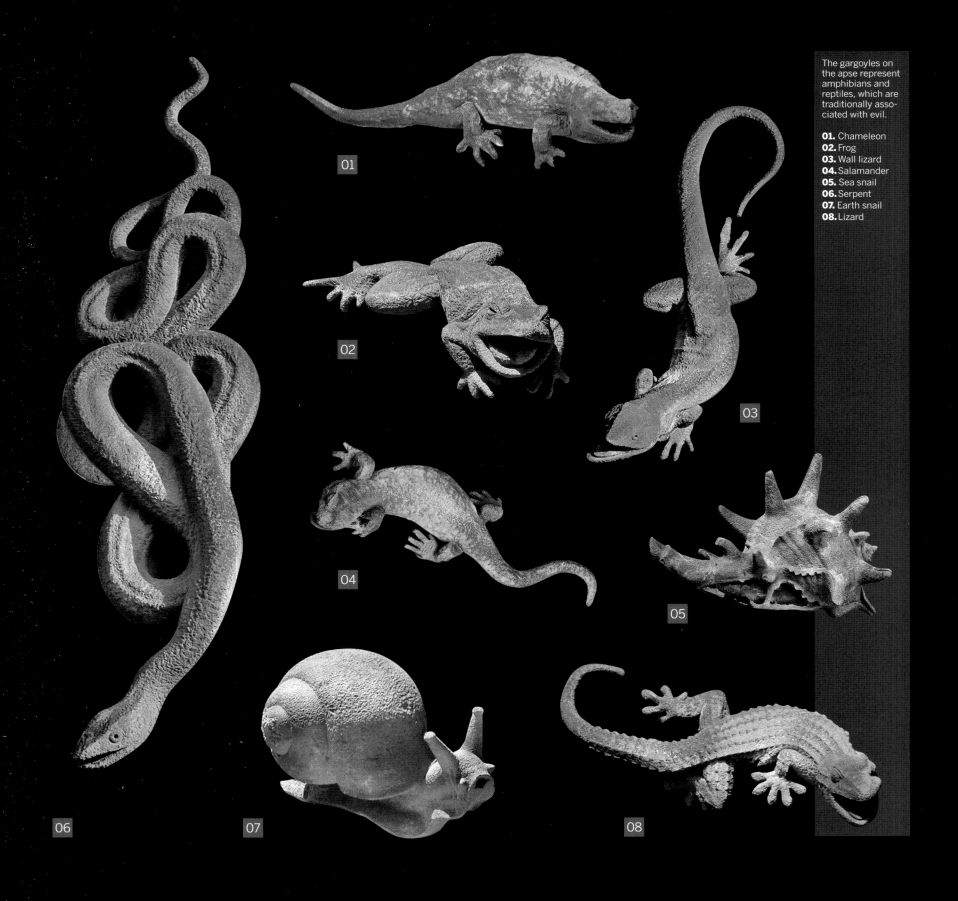

The gargoyles on the apse represent amphibians and reptiles, which are traditionally associated with evil.

01. Chameleon
02. Frog
03. Wall lizard
04. Salamander
05. Sea snail
06. Serpent
07. Earth snail
08. Lizard

01

02

03

04

05

06

07

08

THE CLOISTER
Designed to isolate the temple from the outside

Another of Gaudí's innovations was to recuperate the real significance of the cloister, which was meant to enclose. In monasteries and cathedrals, the cloister is located on one side and is used to provide access to other buildings. Gaudí's cloister surrounds the Sagrada Familia temple and is not only a place for prayer and religious processions, but also prevents street noise from entering.

Towards unity

The function of the cloister, designed by Gaudí, was to unify the different areas and spaces of the Sagrada Familia. It encloses the temple within a 240 metre long rectangular extension, whose four sides correspond with the four façades. The Nativity, Glory and Passion portals break up its continuity. Four magnificent ornamental doorways were planned to maintain unity and to permit access through the façades. Meanwhile, the cloister is located at temple level and the difference in floor level with street level is taken advantage of by the construction of another floor.

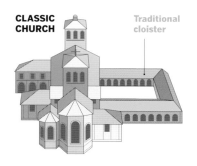

CLASSIC CHURCH
Traditional cloister

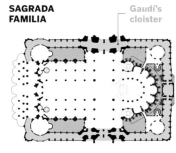

SAGRADA FAMILIA
Gaudí's cloister

1890
THE FIRST SOLUTION FOR THE WALLS
Gaudí planned the walls with frontons decorated with rose windows, which would hold stained glass at a later date.

1919
THE SECOND SOLUTION FOR THE WALLS
Antoni Gaudí simplified the windows by making an equilateral triangle comprised of ten circular holes.

The cloister of the temple

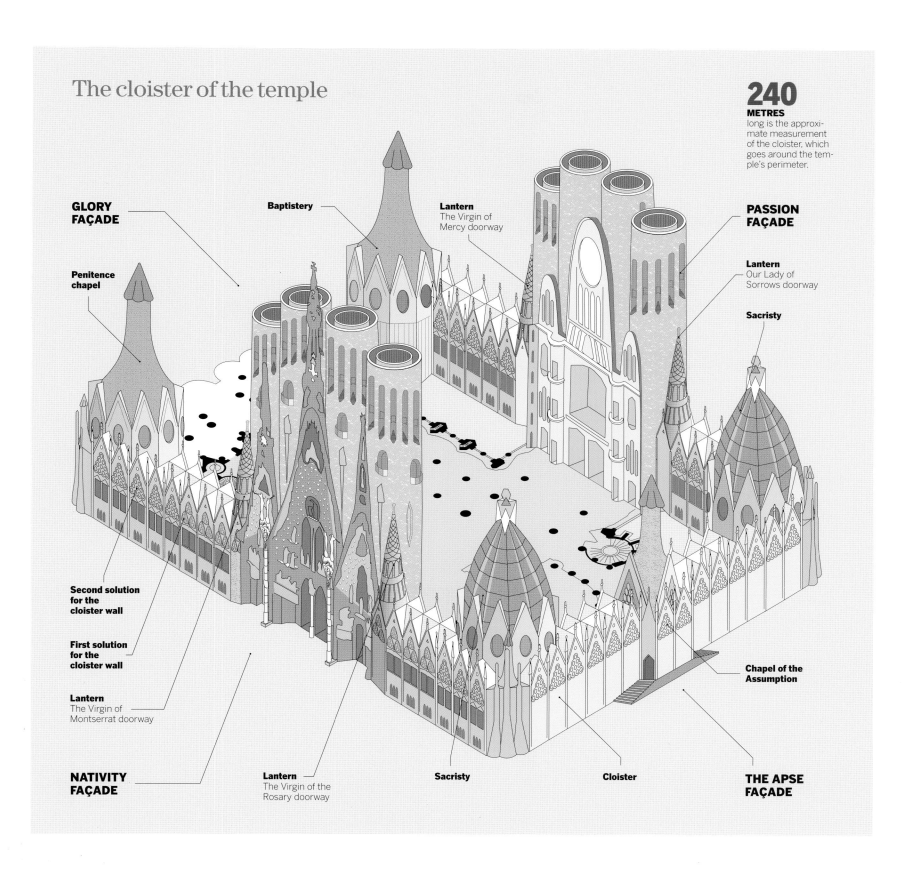

GLORY FAÇADE

Penitence chapel

Baptistery

Lantern
The Virgin of Mercy doorway

PASSION FAÇADE

Lantern
Our Lady of Sorrows doorway

Sacristy

Second solution for the cloister wall

First solution for the cloister wall

Lantern
The Virgin of Montserrat doorway

Chapel of the Assumption

NATIVITY FAÇADE

Lantern
The Virgin of the Rosary doorway

Sacristy

Cloister

THE APSE FAÇADE

THE ROSARY PORTAL

Gaudí chose this portal to show the architects who would carry on with his work how the interior decoration of the temple should be. Roses, in honour of the Virgin to whom the doorway is dedicated, inundate the area.

A doorway full of roses

Each time the cloister intersects with a façade there is a doorway dedicated to the Virgin. Those that are situated on both sides of the Nativity façade are dedicated to the Montserrat and Rosary Virgin. On the Passion façade, will be the Virgin of Mercy and Our Lady of Sorrows doorways. On the Rosary one, the cupola stands out illuminating all the doorway. All the architectonic elements, such as walls, vaults and arches, are decorated with a multitude of roses sculpted in stone with the precision of bobbin lace.

Rosaries
The walls are decorated with rosaries which are sculpted with great realism.

The Virgin of the Rosary
The doorway is presided over by the Virgin with child. At their sides are Saint Domingo and Saint Catalina.

✳

The Rosary Portal
The sculptor Etsuro Sotoo was in charge of sculpting in stone almost all of the sculptures on the portal, given that the original ones were destroyed in the Civil War.

The portal before the Civil War
In front of the doorway is the baptismal font, which is now gone.

01
Cupola of the Rosary Portal
Despite its small dimensions, the portal is extremely well illuminated due to its cupola which provides a lot of light.

 02
Rose decoration
The explosion of roses, which flood the portal, stem from the figure of the Virgin of the Rosary, situated on the tympanum of the doorway.

03
The Death of Just
The Virgin, accompanied by Joseph, shows the child Jesus to a suffering man who clasps a rosary in his hand.

 04
Phrases on the cupola cloister
Amongst olive leaves the last words of the Ave Maria are sculpted in Latin: *Et in hora mortis nostrae. Amen.*

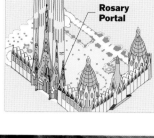

Rosary Portal

The lantern
The cupola is topped by a scaled conical lantern supported by eight leaning columns, which at the same time are sustained by sixteen stone pillars.

01

The stained glass
In the upper part of the cloister there is a numerous quantity of circular windows which are decorated with colourful motifs.

Isaac and Jacob
On each side of the door are sculptures of figures from the Old Testament: The kings David and Solomon and the prophets Isaac and Jacob.

The Holy Family
This symbol is comprised of Jesus' cross, Joseph the carpenter's saw, and Mary's initial.

02

03

04

01

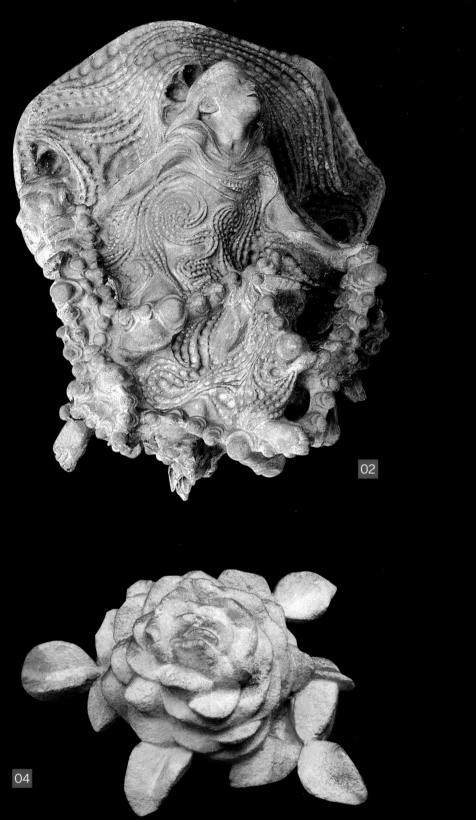

02

03

04

05

THE ASSUMPTION CHAPEL AND THE SACRISTIES

Both projects are distinguished by their original architecture

For the stretch of cloister that runs along the north wing of the temple, Gaudí planned a chapel dedicated to the Assumption of the Virgin and two large sacristies situated on the vertices. These buildings carry a heavy symbolic load and the unmistakeable stamp of their creator: the chapel resembles an enormous stone bed and the sacristies have an original twelve-sided cupola.

The Chapel of the Assumption of the Virgin

In the central part of the cloister, on the apse façade is a small chapel of squared base measuring about 30 metres high, which one can obtain access to from outside, by means of two staircases. When designing this chapel, dedicated to the Assumption of the Virgin Mary, known popularly as the August Virgin whose festivity is celebrated throughout Catalonia, Gaudí was inspired by the funerary bed on which the Virgin is carried in a procession from the Cathedral of Girona. Within the chapel he reproduced all the elements of which the bed is comprised: the curtains, the crown with cross, the pillars and the angels.

Section
The chapel interior will be decorated with representations of the Virgin's attributes.

Access
The chapel, of squared base, is near to the pavement, with stairways leading to the entrance.

The project
Measuring 30 metres high, the lantern is topped with a crown and its four sides are decorated with angels. The façade is presided over by the figure of the Virgin.

Drawing of the chapel
Drawing of exterior, original by Antoni Gaudí.

The Assumption
The August Virgin in Girona cathedral is by the sculptor Bonifàs and inspired Gaudí in the design of the chapel.

The project for the sacristies

The sacristies

Gaudí positioned the sacristies on either side of the Chapel of the Assumption. They comprise of twelve-sided buildings, which are covered over by a cupola and perforated by triangular windows. These windows, along with twelve rose windows in the gallery frontons, guaranteed Gaudí an excellent illumination in the interior.

Cross-section and view of sacristy

The sacristies planned by Gaudí were six floors high, which is the equivalent of a height of 35 metres above street level.

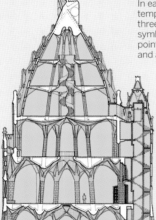
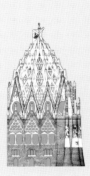

The obelisks

In each corner of the temple there will be three obelisks: each trio symbolizing a cardinal point, a cardinal virtue and a Christian fasting.

The plan view solution

Gaudí engraved the drawing of the plan view on a stone in order to carry out studies on the sacristy.

Sacristy tower

In detailed studies of the sacristies' construction, numerous three-dimensional representations on computer have been made.

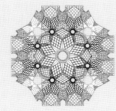

✳ The symbolism

The cupola is decorated with mosaics and palms and finished off with a figure of a grape picker and a lamb, symbols of Jesus Christ.

35 METRES

is the height planned for the sacristy by Gaudí. The base measures 18 by 18 metres.

01

King Solomon
Rosary Portal.

02

King David
Rosary Portal.

03

The Holy Family
This symbol is comprised of Jesus' cross, Joseph the carpenter's saw, and Mary's initial.

04

Mary's sign
The keystone of the cloister window shows the classic anagram of the Virgin Mary: her initial and the ducal crown.

05

The cloister
Second solution for the cloister that Gaudí designed in the year 1919. Its forms are in keeping with the latter architectonic period of Gaudí.

06

Apse pinnacle
One of the apse pinnacles where Jesus' sign is depicted. Behind, the phrases on the bell towers.

07

The Virgin of the Rosary and the child Jesus
Generous decorations of roses sculpted in stone adorn the portico.

08

Cloister vault
Gaudí's neo-gothic symmetry is clearly evident on one of the cloister's vaults.

05

THE NATIVITY FAÇADE

THE TRIUMPH OF LIFE

Tender and joyful, this façade depicts the most human side of Jesus. A great celebration of Creation, in which all living beings rejoice at the birth of the Messiah.

The Nativity façade is also called *La Vida* (Life), *El Gozo* (Joy) and *La Natividad* (Christmas), given that it is an explosion of happiness on the birth of Jesus. The stone seems to lose its static appearance to convey the triumph of life with its own natural forms. This great stone nativity scene carries the message of Hope: The monument appears to herald: Jesus has been born, "Saviour of Mankind". Nature is shown in all its splendour and effervescen-

ce, as Christ's birth supposes the liberation of all life forms. On this spectacular façade, of World Heritage interest, the main events in Jesus' childhood and adolescence are depicted by means of sculptural groups: from the Annunciation up to his conversation in the Temple with the scholars about the Holy Scriptures, on to the flight to Egypt to his presentation in the Temple. The whole façade exudes a great tenderness, particularly in its portrayal of the most human

and familiar facets of Jesus, such as when the adolescent worked alongside and assisted Saint Joseph in his carpentry workshop. To create a greater sensation of proximity and naivety, Gaudí turned to popular elements, such as domestic animals and tools, which the public could easily relate to. However, as with all of Gaudí's works, symbols of great complexity can also be found on this façade with which he sought to reach a higher transcendental plain.

THE NATIVITY FAÇADE

Gaudí chose it to show off the potential of the temple

Gaudí wanted the Nativity façade to be the first one built to demonstrate all the plastic strength that could be achieved by the temple. Work on the foundations commenced in February, 1894 and construction spanned the first third of the 20th century. Once the four bell towers were finished in 1929 and the portal pinnacles completed in 1932, there were only some sculptures left to be done, which were then worked on over the years by various sculptors.

The three porticos

The Nativity façade is comprised of three porticos and four bell towers. The porticos are dedicated to three theological virtues, which are each related to a member of the Holy Family. The central portico, the highest of all, is dedicated to Charity, whose maximum exponent is Jesus. The portico on the right-hand side is dedicated to Faith and devoted to Mary. Lastly, the portico on the left is that of Hope, whose best exponent was Saint Joseph. These three porticos form a unique monument which is set off by the three sculpted figures.

CHRONOLOGY
EVOLUTION OF A FAÇADE

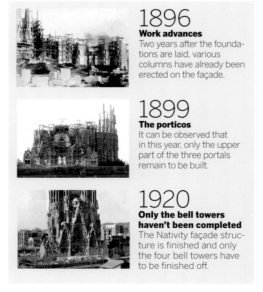

1896
Work advances
Two years after the foundations are laid, various columns have already been erected on the façade.

1899
The porticos
It can be observed that in this year, only the upper part of the three portals remain to be built.

1920
Only the bell towers haven't been completed
The Nativity façade structure is finished and only the four bell towers have to be finished off.

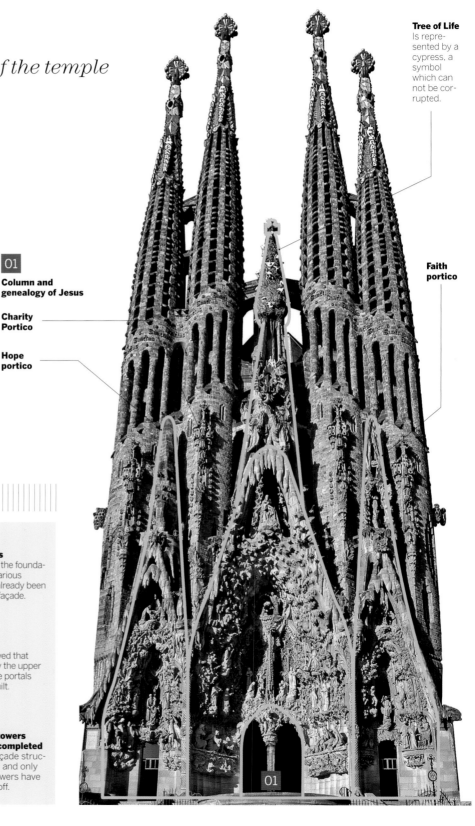

Tree of Life
Is represented by a cypress, a symbol which can not be corrupted.

01
Column and genealogy of Jesus

Charity Portico

Hope portico

Faith portico

01

The columns

The two big columns that are separating the porticos are of great height and finely carved. On the base of each one there is a stone turtle, which symbolizes the unalterable and never changes with time. As for the shanks of the columns they are carved with upwardly spiralling grooves while the capitals are palm leaves from which surge bunches of dates covered in snow, acting as support to the four angel trumpeters who announce the Birth of the Baby Jesus to the four winds.

Palms
The capitals of the columns are formed by groups of palm leaves.

Joseph's inscription
Carved in stone, it is situated on the left column of the Charity portal.

Mary's column
Dedicated to the Virgin, it separates the Charity portico from the Faith Portico.

✳
Trumpeting angels
With their bronze trumpets, the angels announce the Birth of Jesus.

1899
TRUMPETING ANGELS ARE POSITIONED on the façade columns. Gaudí used three soldiers playing the trumpets as models. The fourth model was Ricard Opisso, who collaborated with the architect.

The column of Joseph
Is the one which separates the Hope Portal (dedicated to Saint Joseph) from the Charity Portal (devoted to Jesus).

The sculptures

Gaudí took photographs to study the scenes to be represented. Once the model and posture had been chosen, a plaster cast was taken from the body. This process involved the collaboration of sculptors, Carles Maní, Llorenç Matamala and son Joan, amongst others.

Llorenç Matamala
This Catalan artist worked for years on sculptures with Antoni Gaudí.

✳
The sculpture workshop
Gaudí and his team of sculptors did various studies and tests before definitively carrying out the structures.

Turtle

Tortoise

The turtles
The column located on the mountain side is supported by a tortoise, while the coastal side is supported by a turtle.

Chameleon. Faith portico.

Hope portico.

Chameleons
In contrast to the turtle and tortoise which represent permanence, on either side of the façade is a chameleon which symbolizes change.

01
Construction on the façade, in 1897
The construction work on the façade was carried out at the same time as the work on the sculptures, which would be placed in their appropriate positions as time went on.

02
Model
To carry out the sculptures, Gaudí photographed the model using a mirror system by which the image could be seen from various angles at the same time.

03
The façade interior, 1906
A group of children contemplate the scene.

04
The façade in 1927

05
Sculpture workshop
To arrive at the definitive sculpture, various plaster models were made.

06
Jesus working
Study of sculpture made in plaster.

07
Flight to Egypt
Study of Mary's attire.

08
Skeletons
Gaudí used a life-size skeleton to study the posture of the character to be represented.

09
Sculpture workshop
In the foreground, the Flight to Egypt yet to be finished.

THE CHARITY PORTICO

The central portico, which is also called Love, is the largest on the façade. Built as if it were an enormous cave, within it are the characters that were present at the Birth of Jesus.

The adoration of the shepherds

The shepherds and the animals look on at the newly born Jesus with great tenderness, moved by having found the son of God. They were the first to see the star of Bethlehem and to worship the Baby Jesus. They symbolize the people.

The Adoration of the Kings

Melchior, Caspar and Balthazar, the Three Wise Men from the Orient and guided by the Star of Bethlehem, introduced themselves to Jesus with offerings of gold, frankincense and myrrh.

The dog
As well as a popular figure, it symbolizes loyalty.

The lamb
Represents innocence and docility. It was a gift from the shepherds to Jesus.

Pedestal detail
As in a nativity scene, the pedestals of the Adoration of the Shepherds and the Three Wise Men are covered with a large variety of birds and plants.

The Coronation of Mary

Topping the portico, this amazing work by Joan Matamala, according to Gaudí's project, depicts the moment when the Virgin was crowned as reward for her self-sacrificing love to God.

Saint Joseph
In the Catholic tradition, the Holy Trinity crowns the Virgin. In this group, Saint Joseph substitutes God and a third man substitutes the Holy Spirit.

Jesus
Jesus blesses the Virgin Mary, and crowns her Queen and Empress of Heaven and Earth.

The Virgin Mary

The Holy Spirit

The Annunciation of Mary

The sculptural group, situated between the groups of the Coronation of Mary and the angel musicians, shows the moment in which the archangel Gabriel informs a submissive and devoted Mary, that she has been chosen to be the Mother of the Son of God. The scene is completed with a rosary and numerous birds breaking out of the stone.

The rosary. The fifty-nine beads of the rosary go round the window.

The birds. With dynamism, groups of birds emanate from the stone.

COLUMN AND DOORWAY OF JESUS

On the lower part of the Charity Portico is a column of spiral form, which is carved in relief and details the family tree of Jesus. This pillar supports the Holy Family, which is represented in the sculptural group on the Nativity.

The stone nativity
The child Jesus rests in the manger, accompanied by Joseph and Mary. Around them the child angels sing in chorus to celebrate the Birth of the Son of the God.

The Nativity
The recently born Jesus protected by Joseph and Mary rests on the column capital. Completing this scene, are also the ox and mule, symbolic of the Messiah's humbleness. All the sculptural and architectonic elements of the façade are arranged so that the viewer's attention is focused on the baby Jesus figure.

Gloria in excelsis Deus...
Inscribed in Latin on the upper part of the doors is, *Glory to God on high and on earth peace to all men of goodwill*, which is the phrase the angels said to the shepherds on the announcement of the Birth of Jesus.

1958
WAS THE YEAR
when the sculptural group on the Nativity, by sculptor Joan Busquets, was put into place.

Squirrel and flower
All over the Nativity façade there are numerous references to Nature. Their purpose is to convey the joy evoked at the birth of the Messiah.

The phrase
Two angels, on the doorway lintel, support an inscription, which reads: *Jesus est natus. Venite, adoremus.*

Chorus of baby angels

Situated around the sculptural group on the Nativity façade, the original angel chorus sculptures, designed by Gaudí, were made of plaster and were destroyed during the Civil War. The sculptures that now appear are carved in stone and are an interpretation by the Japanese sculptor, Etsuro Sotoo, carried out based on the ideas that Gaudí left behind.

The sculptor Etsuro Sotoo
Dazzled by Antoni Gaudí's work, he has been collaborating with the sculptures on the Sagrada Familia since 1978.

The column of Jesus

Located in the centre of the portico and dividing it into two, the column represents the genealogy of Jesus by means of a winding carved ribbon. On the base there is a serpent biting the apple, symbolic of the original sin, which was the reason why Jesus came to Earth. On the capital, a delicate carving in stone gives the column its name.

The inscription of Jesus

The snake and the apple

01

Zodiac signs
The constellations of the Zodiac are represented such as they were seen on the night Jesus was born.

02

The adoration of Caspar
In his bowl he brings incense on Jesus' birth.

03

Charity Portico
Simulating an enormous nativity scene, the sculptural group of the Birth of Jesus dominates the scene.

04

The Birth of Jesus
Mary protects the newly-born Jesus.

05

The gift from the shepherds
A shepherd offers a present of a basket laden with eggs.

06

Domestic animals

07

The star of Bethlehem
Announces the Birth of Jesus.

08

The Column of Jesus
A ribbon wrapped around the column shows Jesus Christ's genealogy.

01

02

THE HOPE PORTICO

With this portico Gaudí reunited the childhood situations of Jesus that better embody Joseph and his virtue, hope.

The rocky outcrop of Montserrat
The pinnacle topping the portico seems to be an allegory of the mountain of Montserrat. Written on it is: *Sálvanos.*

Saint Joseph's boat
Saint Joseph appears as the helmsman who led the Catholic church, which is symbolized by the boat. The figure of Saint Joseph looks very much like Gaudí, given that, supposedly, it was the tribute that the temple workers paid to him after his death.

The anchor and the lamp
The large sized lamp, is used to light up the pathway of the Church.

Escape to Egypt
Shortly after the departure of the Three Wise Men, an angel warns Joseph of the danger of staying in Bethlehem. During the night, the Holy Family flee to Egypt with Jesus to escape the hands of King Herod's soldiers. An angel, with energetic attitude, pulls on an ass, which is ridden by the Virgin with baby Jesus in her arms.

The raised ass
In order to carry out the figure of the ass of the Flight to Egypt, Gaudí made a cast from a live donkey. In order that the animal wouldn't move around during the casting it was hoisted up in the air during the process.

Domestic animals
The geese or ducks on the lower part are an allusion to the Nile's aquatic fauna.

Rosary and tools
Gaudí combined the holy (the rosary) with the everyday, personified by the great variety of tools sculpted.

The Massacre of the Innocents

With great dramatic force, this event is presented by a soldier of enormous dimensions who on the point of killing a new born baby is unperturbed by the pleading cries of its mother.

1935
THEY FINISHED
work on the last sculptures, completing work on the Hope portico that concluded 35 years of study and construction.

The betrothal of the Virgin Mary and Saint Joseph

In this depiction Mary and Joseph are shown in the temple, which is decorated for the occasion with roses and palm leaves, at the moment when a priest joins them in matrimony. There are also various angels present who assist the priest in his duties.

Jesus's family

Jesus shows an injured dove to his father, while his moved grandparents Saint Joachim and Saint Anne look on.

01

The Innocent Saints
A Roman soldier tries to kill an innocent baby.

02

Death of the Innocents
A baby lays dead at the feet of a soldier.

03

Nile birds and plants
Pedestal base of the sculptural group from the Flight to Egypt.

04

The Innocent Saints
A mother pleads for her son to a Roman soldier.

05

Mary detail
The Virgin carrying baby Jesus on the Flight to Egypt.

06

Tools
On the lintel of the doorway appear a large quantity of tools, such as a carpenter's brush and a ruler.

07

Dragonfly
Nile flora and fauna are present all over the portal.

THE FAITH PORTICO

This portico is dedicated to the Faith and the Virgin Mary who is maximum exponent of this virtue. Some of the most significant scenes from Jesus' childhood and adolescence in the Gospel are depicted here.

Jesus working

Situated on the right-hand side of the portico, this sculpture of great realism represents a young Jesus aiding Joseph in his carpentry workshop in Nazareth.

The sculpture process
Once the plaster cast mould was made, the figure was adjusted and then attired. Later, it was made into its real size and if the desired effect was obtained then it was carved in stone.

Joseph and Mary

With a mix of adoration and surprise, they observe their son while he explains to the doctors in the Temple the exact sense of the Holy Scriptures.

Jesus the worker
A symbol of work, a worker bee is on the head of Jesus.

Jesus preaches in the Temple

Jesus was only aged twelve when he explained the exact sense of the Holy Scriptures to the scholars in the Temple. At his side is his cousin Saint John the Baptist, who would later be his precursor and most beloved disciple.

Saint John the Baptist, Jesus and Zachariah
The figure on the right is Zachariah, the father of Jesus' cousin, Saint John the Baptist who is on the left. Jesus the central figure preaches in the Temple.

Wheats
Placed on the pinnacle that tops the Faith Portico and 54 metres high above street level, grapes and wheatears symbolize the wine and bread shared out in the Eucharist.

Providence
Divine Providence is represented by the hand that guides and the eye that sees.

The Immaculate Conception
Recalls the Catholic Church dogma which advocates that the Virgin was conceived without the original sin.

The proportions

The Visitation
The Virgin Mary visits her cousin Elisabeth to tell her that she is expecting the Messiah. Thus, Saint Elisabeth becomes witness to the mystery of the Incarnation.

Optical distortion
Gaudí increased the height of the figures high-up so that they would be viewed the same as the figures low-down.

Jesus in Simon's arms
Satisfying Hebrew law, Joseph and Mary present their child in the Temple, where he is blessed by the priest Simon.

Mary's anagram
It is comprised of her name's initial and a star, a symbol identifying the Virgin as the light which precedes the coming of Christ.

Three-pointed lamp
On the upper part of the portico, the Virgin is standing on a pedestal that represents a three-pointed lamp, symbol of the Holy Trinity.

The Heart of Jesus
The heart, the most human representation of Jesus, is covered by thorns and mystic bees which feed on his blood.

THE TREE OF LIFE

The most representative pinnacle of the Nativity façade is the symbolic compendium of the three porticos: it represents the triumph of the life and legacy of Jesus.

The Pelican

This bird was a symbol that was widely used by the first Christians to represent the ceremony of the Eucharist. In those times it was believed that the pelican would open its breast in order to feed its baby chicks as a sign of motherhood and protection.

Holy Trinity

The pinnacle is crowned with the Greek letter *tau*, God's initial in the Greek language; the cross, Jesus' symbol, and the dove which is identified with the Holy Spirit. In this manner, the Holy Trinity is represented.

Stairs

The two stairs leaning on the cypress represent aspiration to reach God.

The cypress

This tree symbolizes eternal life for its resistant wood and its evergreen leaves.

Jesus' anagram

The letters *JHS* derived from Jesus Christ come from the Latin, *Jesuschristus*. The initials are on a cross, at whose sides are the Greek letters *alpha* and *omega*. This anagram symbolizes that the Cross, in other words Jesus, is the beginning and the end of everything.

21
DOVES
are sheltering in the Tree of Life. They were originally sculpted in alabaster, but in 1990 were replaced by ones carved in marble.

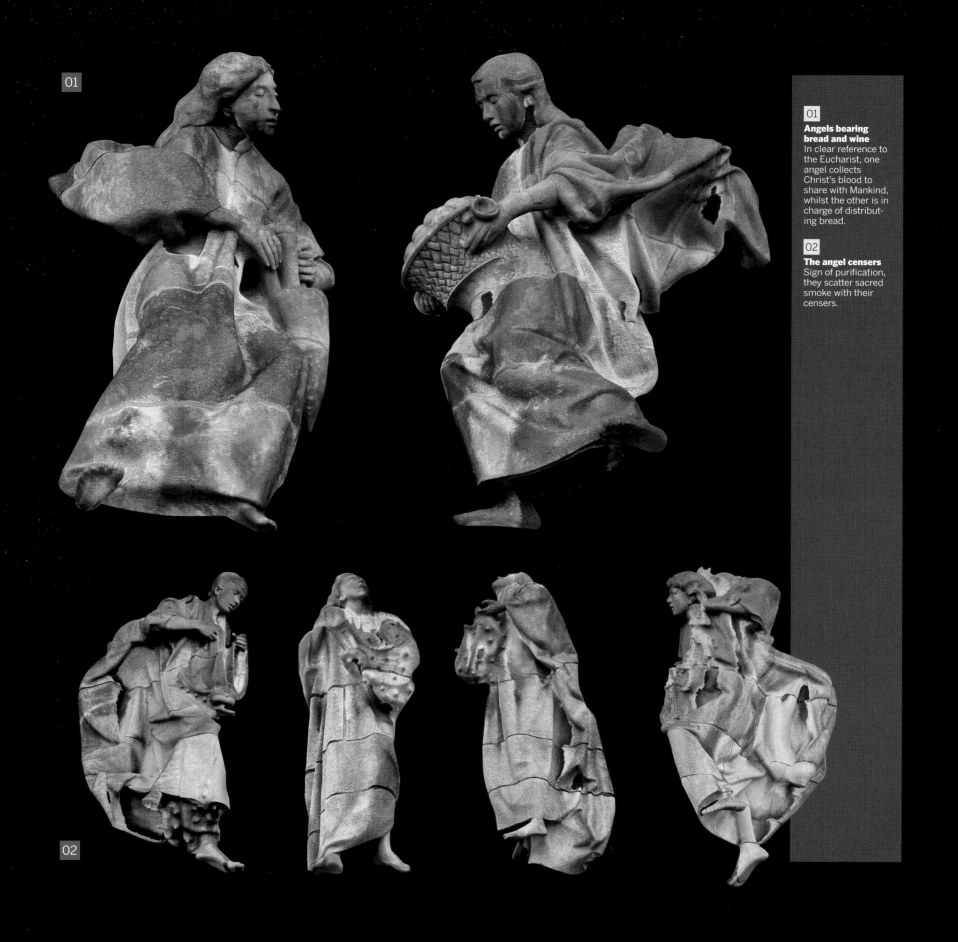

01

01

Angels bearing bread and wine
In clear reference to the Eucharist, one angel collects Christ's blood to share with Mankind, whilst the other is in charge of distributing bread.

02

The angel censers
Sign of purification, they scatter sacred smoke with their censers.

02

 01
Domestic animals
Pedestal of the sculptural group of Jesus working.

 02
Simon
While holding Jesus, Simon says to Mary: "He has been put here for the fall and rise of many in Israel…"

03
Anne, Fanuel's daughter
The prophet Anne, of advanced age, was present at the ceremony and told everybody of the Birth of the Messiah.

04
Vegetable details
Pedestal of sculptural group of the Visitation of Mary.

05
Jesus carpenter
A young Jesus works in Joseph's workshop.

06
The Holy Trinity

07
The dove
White doves shelter in the Tree of Life.

08
Trumpeting angel
In the background, sculptural group of the presentation of Jesus in the Temple.

06

THE PASSION FAÇADE

THE REPRESENTATION OF DEATH

Sparse decoration with sculptures of hard schematic forms, this façade conveys Christ's suffering during the last days of his life.

When observing the Passion façade, a certain perception of coldness and sadness is unavoidable. For this is what it strives to achieve, to show the suffering or the Passion of Christ and his death. Gaudí was conscious of the impact that this portal would have on the citizens, which was why he decided to start its construction once the Nativity façade had been completed. By doing so, he avoided popular rejection and gained more leeway in order that the global

message of the temple would be understood. To convey this idea of desolation and pain, Gaudí freed the façade from any type of ornamentation. Likewise, he simplified its structure leaving clean hard bone-like shapes, with no more adornment than the cold nudity of the stone. The reason for this absence of decoration is so that attention is primarily paid to the groups of sculptures that describe the last days in the life of Jesus. The whole portal functions as an enormous stage where the

most relevant events in the Passion of Jesus Christ unfold in chronological order before the viewer's eyes. Responsible for the execution of the sculptures on this façade is Josep Maria Subirachs. This Catalan sculptor has interpreted the material that Gaudí left behind imprinting, on the façade's sculptures, an austere and nude line. His work is characterised by its angled and schematic forms, whose marked profiles help to underline the drama of the monument.

THE PASSION FAÇADE
Pain and sacrifice sculpted in stone

In contrast to the optimism and vitality exuded by the decorative exuberance of the Nativity façade, the Passion façade expresses the pain and anguish of Jesus Christ's death with austerity and harshness.

West-facing, where the sun sets every day, this façade recalls the cruelty of sacrifice by means of a series of sculptural groups that represent the last days in the life of Jesus up until his death.

The Passion according to Gaudí

In 1911, Gaudí withdrew to the locality of Puigcerdà to recover from a life-threatening illness. Inspired by his own suffering, he set upon planning the Passion façade, on which he wanted to imprint all the hardness of sacrifice. Gaudí left behind a variety of drawings, studies and sketches of how the structure and decoration should be. It was in 1954 that work commenced on the façade according to Gaudí's project, consisting of a portico supported by six leaning columns, over which 18 small bone-shaped columns sustain a huge frontage. This frontage is the last thing of all to be built on the Passion façade monument.

The Passion façade
The sculptor Subirachs made the order of the scenes, from the Last Supper to the Burial, follow an "S" shape to reproduce the path that Jesus followed on the road to Calvary.

First sketch of the façade
Gaudí's first proposal for the Passion façade was very similar in structure and imagery to that of the Nativity façade.

How to view the sculptures
The dotted line indicates the sequence to follow when viewing the sculptures.

Upper level

Middle level

Lower level

1957 **The foundations.** Work is carried out on the façade bases.

1960 **The façade.** Work commences on the construction of the first walls.

1965 **Work commences.** The façade reaches a height of 11 metres.

1969 **The portico.** Work is done on the columns, which reach 12 metres.

Original drawing by Gaudí, 1911
When Gaudí explained the project for the Passion façade, he said: "Someone might find this façade too extravagant, but I wanted it to frighten, and on doing so I won't skimp on the chiaroscuro..."

The Ascension of Christ
The façade is crowned by a bronze sculpture measuring 5 metres high and weighing 2000 kilos.

Subirachs, the sculptor
In 1986, the artist Josep Maria Subirachs started on the execution of the sculptural groups on the façade. After dedicating a year to the study of Gaudí's work, Subirachs commenced sculpting in 1987 and from this moment, just like Gaudí did, he was fully dedicated to a task which has become the most important work of his life. As his sculptures show, Subirachs is defined as an extremely cerebral sculptor.

Tree-like columns
To sustain the weight of the portico Gaudí dreamt up enormous leaning columns, similar to the trunk of the conifer tree, the sequoia. These monumental masses of stone, add to the monument's feeling of nudity and desolation.

The reference
With great exactitude the shape of the column was made to coincide with that of a tree.

1954 CONSTRUCTION COMMENCES
on the Passion façade, after many years of reconstructing and studying Gaudí's drawings, plans and models.

THE LAST NIGHT OF JESUS

In this area of the Passion façade are depicted the main events that Jesus experienced during his last night: ranging from the dinner with the apostles up until his arrest by the Roman soldiers.

The Last Supper

Put into position in 1994, it is the first sculptural group on the Passion monument and nearest to the spectator. It is placed on the left-hand side of the façade and depicts the moment when Jesus, sitting at a table amongst his disciples, asks Judas Iscariot, who is on the point of abandoning the scene with his hand closed as if hiding something, to betray him as quickly as possible. Apart from Jesus and Judas, Saint John also stands out from the group, Jesus' favourite disciple, who deeply affected, rests his head on his arm.

Saint John
He was the disciple chosen by Subirachs to show the apostles' grief.

The dog
Belongs to The Last Supper group. It is interpreted as loyalty or indifference to betrayal.

Peter and the soldiers

This is the moment when Peter tried to stop the soldiers from taking Jesus away. In his struggle with the soldiers, Peter cuts off the ear of Malco, the High Priest's servant. The apostle only gives up the fight with the guard when Jesus says; "Those who wield the sword, will perish at the sword".

Malco's ear
On the trunk of an olive tree is a drawing of the temple guardian's ear cut off by Peter.

Peter asleep
When Judas betrays his Master, Peter is asleep. On hearing the soldiers, he draws his sword to defend Jesus. The apostle is represented as a rock, in allusion to his name and the mission commended by Jesus: "You will be the rock on which my church will be built".

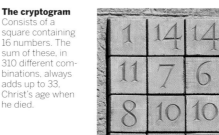

Mark, 14:45
It is the verse in the Bible that tells of the betrayal: "And when he came, he approached him, and he said: Master, Master. And he kissed him".

The kiss of Judas

Sealing his betrayal, Judas kisses Jesus to indicate whom his master is to the soldiers who lie in wait, awaiting the signal to arrest him. This scene took place at night, on the Mount of Olives. In order to show more effectively how these people would have been viewed in the dark, the sculptor Subirachs decided not to clearly define the outlines of the sculpted figures.

The cryptogram
Consists of a square containing 16 numbers. The sum of these, in 310 different combinations, always adds up to 33, Christ's age when he died.

The serpent
Traditionally associated with evil and in this case being the devil's symbol that inspired the disciple to betray Christ. For this reason it is placed behind the figure of Judas.

THE DENIAL AND THE TRIAL

The two scenes that describe the facts that would be decisive for the future of Jesus are situated on the lower right-hand side of the façade: the visit to the house of the High Priest and the trial held by Pontius Pilate.

Peter and his denial

Peter denied knowing his master on three occasions; his posture and facial expression reflect the shame he feels for his actions. As a metaphor of his denial, the apostle appears swathed in a sheet and three women represent his three denials. One of them points at him indicating that he was one of Jesus' disciples.

The cockerel
As was predicted, Peter denies that he knows Jesus before the cockerel cries announcing the dawn of a new day.

The labyrinth. It is a symbol recuperated from medieval cathedrals which recalls Jesus' path after his capture.

01
Ecce Homo
After being beaten, Jesus is presented before the people wearing a crown of thorns. The governor Pilate is sitting down overwhelmed by the decision he has to make. The stone cracks under Jesus' feet.

02
The Roman eagle
Is situated on the column whose inscription reads: *Tiberius, emperor of Rome.*

03
The trial of Jesus
Pilate washes his hands; with this gesture the governor abstains from deciding Christ's destiny.

04
Claudia Prócula
Pilate's wife abandons the scene distressed by the situation, after warning her husband "Don't get involved in the affair of this just man: for today in my dreams I have suffered for his cause."

01

The Last Supper
Sitting at the centre of the table, Jesus says to Judas: "What you are going to do, do it soon".

02 03

The apostles
The stricken apostles at the moment when Jesus informs them he will be betrayed.

04

Pilate
The Roman prosecutor is shown sitting next to Ecce Homo.

05

The denial of Peter
The apostle's grave expression is hidden in his cloak as a sign of his denial of Christ.

06

Secret meeting
Placed on both sides of the façade.

07

Two women who accused Peter of being with Jesus.

THE DOORS

By means of written text, the use of texture and inlays, the sculptor Josep Maria Subirachs used these three doorways that access the temple to convey the general message of the façade.

The Gospel doors

The central doors synthetically symbolize the work on the façade, telling in words what is illustrated by the different sculptural groups. Above them, the Gospel text is reproduced, narrating the last two days in the life of Jesus. This way, the doors, separated by a mullion, function as the pages of a monumental New Testament, which serves as a backdrop to the flagellation figure.

8.000
BRONZE CHARACTERS were cast to write the text on the Gospel doors. Some words of particular significance are polished so that they stand out from the rest.

Alpha and omega Are the first and last letters of the Greek alphabet. They are frequently used Christian symbols that signify that Jesus is the beginning and end of Creation.

The Coronation of Thorns door. Inlay details.

The Coronation of Thorns door. Jesus facing Pilate.

The Gethsemane door. High relief with letters.

The Gethsemane door. The disciples sleep.

The Gethsemane door

The door measures 5.87 metres high and 2.40 metres wide. It is made of bronze and was carried out between 1992 and 1994. The relieves depict Jesus praying in the garden while three of his disciples are asleep. Verses describing this scene are also written.

Subirach's homage to Gaudí

The Coronation of Thorns door

The central relief depicts the humiliation that Jesus suffered at the hands of the Roman soldiers when after his torture; they gave him a crown of thorns and a cane as a sceptre. In the middle part is shown, like a mirror effect, the presentation of Jesus before Herod, on the left-hand side, and before Pilate, on the right. On the surface of the door a quotation from Dante's *Divine Comedy* is engraved along with some verses from a poem by Salvador Espriu.

The sceptre
As a joke he is given a cane as sceptre.

The crown
The soldiers crown him with thorns.

THE FLAGELLATION OF CHRIST

This sculpture depicts Jesus, alone, tied to a column after being tortured by Roman soldiers.

The flagellation

This event is one of the most dramatic moments of the Passion of Christ, given that Jesus is completely alone during his flagellation. Not one of his disciples or his family are there, with only his torturers surrounding him. To convey with greater vehemence this terrible feeling of solitude, the sculpture has been placed between the denial of Peter and the betrayal of Judas. It is the most important figure on the lower level, reaching a height of five metres and is sculpted in travertine marble of the highest quality. Around the sculpture are the instruments that were used during his torture.

The column
Its division into four parts symbolizes the four arms of the cross. It's juxtaposition recalls the end of the ancient world.

The fossil
According to the sculptor, a fossil of a palm leaf was found in the block of marble stone, symbolizing martyrdom.

The cane
It symbolizes psychological torture. It reflects the ridicule that Christ suffered when the soldiers gave him a cane instead of a mitre, a sign of royalty.

The stair
The three steps from which the column rises represent the three days that passed between the crucifixion and the death of Jesus Christ and his Resurrection.

The knot
Sculpted with great realism, the knot symbolizes the physical torture suffered by Christ.

Flagellation of Jesus. It is placed in complete solitude.

GETSEMANÍ

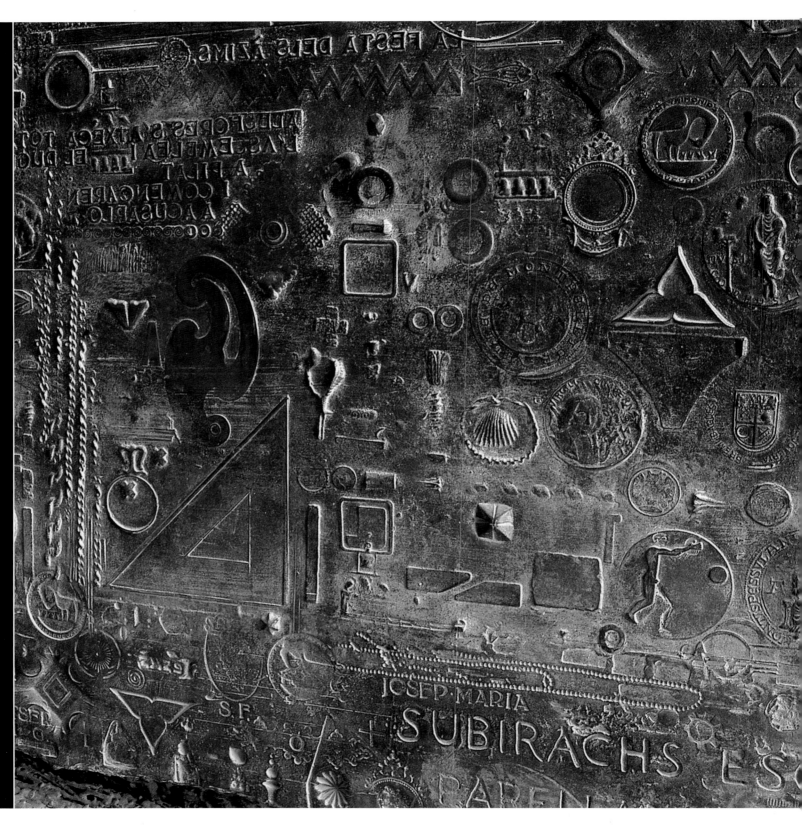

PATH TO THE CRUCIFIXION

Presided over by Christ's face, which is stamped on *Veronica's Veil*, this level represents the path called the *Via Crucis*: the route that Jesus followed laden with the cross, to the mountain of Calvary where he was crucified.

The central group
Representing the second fall of Jesus, this sculptural group is the most numerous on the façade, as it is made up of seventeen figures.

Veronica and the evangelist

Shows Jesus Christ's second falter on the Calvary path. In the middle of the scene Veronica appears showing the veil on which Jesus' face is marked. Her figure has no face in order that more attention is paid to Jesus' face. Here, the sculptor, pays homage to Gaudí: by the evangelist and soldiers' helmets, which represent Casa Milà's chimneys.

Tribute to Gaudí
Subirachs used this photo as a base to represent Gaudí as the evangelist who would tell the story of Jesus.

La Pedrera
In another homage to Antoni Gaudí, Subirachs copied the Roman soldier helmets of the Pedrera chimneys.

Negative image
Is the sculptural way of representing the image of Jesus' face on the veil that Veronica gave him to wipe away his sweat.

01
The three Marys
The three women crying for the fallen Jesus represent the Virgin, Mary of Cleophas and Mary Magdalene.

02
Longinus
Is believed to be the soldier that crossed his lance across Jesus' side on the cross. Afterwards, he converted to Christianity and ended up as a Church martyr.

03
Detail
This figure represents a girl from the group of women from Jerusalem that Jesus encountered on the way to the mountain of Calvary.

04
Simon of Cyrene
Jesus is shown lying on the floor and Simon of Cyrene, forced by the soldiers, helps him raise the cross.

THE CRUCIFIXION AND THE BURIAL

Materializing on this level is the depiction of the death of Jesus on the cross. The central sculptural composition is deliberately asymmetric, complimenting the drama and agony of the scene.

The crucifixion of Jesus

Jesus has now died on the cross. On his left are Mary Magdalene, kneeling, and the Virgin Mary, who is being consoled by John. A little further back is Mary of Cleophas. The cross is made with two iron bars. The front part of the start of the vertical bar is painted the colour red to highlight an "I", the first letter of the inscription I.N.R.I.

Death
This is represented by a solitary skull carved in stone.

The moon
Solitary on one side, it represents the night.

DATA
PROPORTION OF THE ELEMENTS

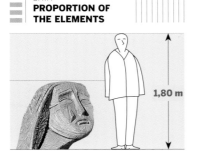

1,80 m

The torn curtain

As if it were an enormous bald-achin, this bronze structure is above the death scene of Jesus on the Cross. It represents the curtain that, according to Hebrew tradition, separated the holiest place in the Temple of Jerusalem from the rest of the rooms. According to the Gospel, this curtain ripped from top to bottom into two pieces as the earth trembled and rocks cracked at the precise moment Jesus died. Through the curtain the upper arch of the central atrium is seen, on which appear a series of inscriptions, letters and drawings in poly-chromatic ceramic work.

01.
Curtain detail
To achieve a fabric style effect, the bronze curtain forms different creases.

02.
Detail of the atrium
On the upper arch strong coloured letters and draw-ings are combined.

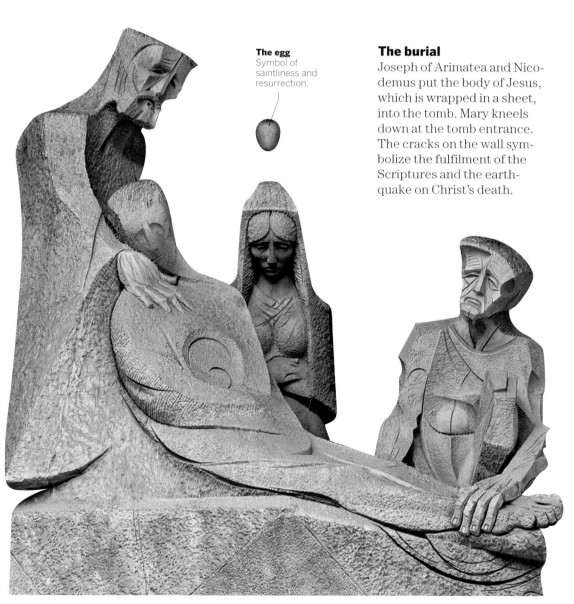

The egg
Symbol of saintliness and resurrection.

The burial

Joseph of Arimatea and Nico-demus put the body of Jesus, which is wrapped in a sheet, into the tomb. Mary kneels down at the tomb entrance. The cracks on the wall sym-bolize the fulfilment of the Scriptures and the earth-quake on Christ's death.

Soldiers playing with dice

Four Roman soldiers are depicted playing for Christ's clothes, while he agonizes on the cross. Three figures are sculpted, while the fourth's helmet can just be made out. The game table is in the shape of a lamb's bone that, it is believed, was the origin of dice. This sculptur-al group occupies the first group on the upper floor, fol-lowing the events of Jesus' last two days alive.

Detail. Shows a soldier's hands.

The helmets
The Pedrera chimneys influ-enced Josep Maria Subirachs.

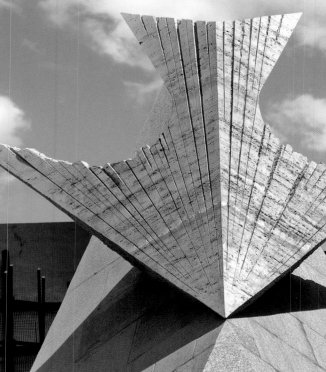

01

The Crucifixion and the Veronica
The sculptural groups on the central part represent the most tragic moments of the death of Jesus.

02

The Holy Spirit
Is represented by an abstract dove, the classic symbol of the Holy Spirit.

03
Mary Magdalene
With deep sadness she contemplates the deceased Jesus.

04
The Ascension of Christ
The façade is crowned by a bronze sculpture measuring 5 metres and weighing 2000 kilos.

05

Jesus fallen
Jesus collapses on the floor, his first fall on the way to Calvary.

06

The Lamb
Done in brightly coloured ceramic work, it symbolizes the resurrection of Jesus.

07
The horse
Close-up view of Longinus' horse.

01

THE GLORY FAÇADE

PRAISE TO GOD

The largest façade on the temple is designed to show Jesus Christ exerting his divinity, invoking the prayer: "Glory to the Father, the Son and the Holy Spirit".

As in many of the great Christian temples, the Sagrada Familia devotes its main façade, whose entrance allows access inside the temple via the central nave, to the representation of the Glory, God's place of reign and where any believer would aspire to reach. This way, it acts as a perfect compliment to the two other façades, which show the earthly facets of Jesus (birth and death), while the Glory façade puts special emphasis on his divine condition. Facing the midday sun, this façade boasts the best orientation and is also the largest, in width and height. Gaudí didn't go into great detail how it should be, only outlining the general shape and studying images and symbols that he felt it ought to contain. From these studies it can be deduced that the architect wanted to bestow the façade with an unmistakeable educational purpose, as with the rest of the temple. Gaudí wanted the spectator to be able to see the complete history of Christian mankind, from Creation to the Final Judgement, just like the path offered by the Church in search of eternal life. In reality, this façade is an enormous catechism on which the pillars of Christianity appear: the most important prayers (the Creed and Our Father), the sacraments, the deadly sins and their opposing virtues, Heaven and Hell. This rich symbolic universe will have its say in an exuberant and majestic architecture, only intuited in the other two façades already built.

THE GLORY FAÇADE
The most important and monumental of all

The Glory façade will show the struggle of Humanity to reach eternal life and each man's journey to attain it. To do this, Gaudí wanted to represent Death, the first unavoidable step; the Final Judgement, presided over by Jesus Christ; the Glory, which is the reward to honourable men; and Hell, divine punishment which God inflicts on those who stray from his laws.

A spectacular entrance

Gaudí didn't tie up all the details of the Glory façade, but he did define, by means of a model, how its ground plan would be and the essence of its structure and its shape. Likewise, he also specified its symbolic and iconographic content which was highly complex and totally Gaudí.
This façade is the monumental frame that Gaudí envisaged for the doorway which would

allow access to the interior of the Sagrada Familia temple. His idea was that, before entering the holy area, the visitor would be conscious of how man was created and what his destiny is in this world. Over the doors, Gaudí imagined huge illuminated clouds which would hang from the bell towers and on which the Creed would be written in large letters: the prayer that sums up the dogma of Christian faith.

Antoni Gaudí

> **Originality mustn't be sought for, as then it is extravagance. One must observe what is usually done and then try to improve on it"**

The model made by Gaudí
The portico is covered by the four bell tower vaults and by sixteen lanterns, which are arranged in ascending order from the sides towards the centre and from the front to behind.

Bell Towers
Are the highest of the three façades. They represent Saint Peter, Saint Paul, Saint Andrew, and Saint James the Greater.

The Creed
The letters of the word *Credo* (Creed) are luminous so that they can be read a long distance away at day or night.

Jesus
To carry out the Final Judgement, Christ appears with attributes from the Passion, surrounded by angels.

Genesis
On the clouds which embrace the lanterns the creation of the world is narrated according to Genesis.

Baptistery
Is decorated with allegories of baptism.

Penitence Chapel

Death
According to the original project, death would be represented by tombs.

The entrance stairs to the temple
A staircase and terrace provide access to the Glory portico.

The Glory façade. The illustrator Berenguer did the drawing of the façade, interpreting the symbolism chosen by Gaudí.

Montserrat mountain
The doorway is inspired by the mountain Montserrat's curious forms.

16
LANTERNS
of different sizes make up the portico.

DATA
URBANISATION STUDY IN THE YEAR 1975

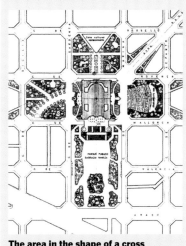

The area in the shape of a cross
According to a proposal in 1975, a garden would be in front of the Glory façade, reaching the Diagonal Avenue. At present, the City Council is working on other urban plans that differ to the cross shape proposal.

THE GLORY PORTICO

The history of man and the pillars of the Christian faith are represented on the Glory portico. All architectonic and decorative elements are at the service of this monumental symbolism.

The portal's symbolism

On the façade every stage of the human being is represented. Above the doors, are Adam and Eve, parents of humanity. Above them are Saint Joseph in his carpentry workshop, surrounded by workers. Higher up, are Faith, Hope and Charity, represented by the Ark of the Covenant, Noah's Ark and the House of Nazareth. The highest place of all, in the central axis, is reserved for the Virgin. Her gaze falls upon Jesus, who is judging Mankind. A great rose window symbolizes the Holy Spirit and above it, at the highest point, soars the majestic image of God the Father.

The trumpeting angels and Noah's Ark are also represented on the portico.

The Glory, **according to Titian.** This is how the painter imagined God's abode heaven, to be.

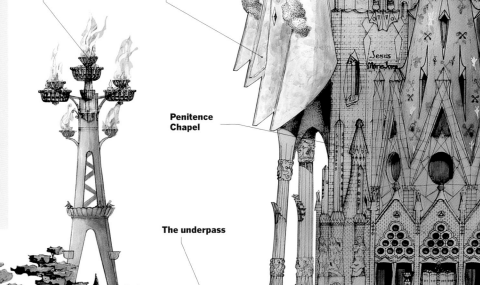

Monument to Fire and Water
Situated in the forecourt of the temple and in front of the Penitence chapel is a monumental torch with different arms, while at the other end, in front of the baptistery is a fountain which spurts water to a great height and represents the four rivers of paradise.

Monument to Fire

The façade lanterns

Penitence Chapel

The underpass

The underpass

In Gaudí's original project, to obtain access to the Glory portal an enormous platform had to be built over the street Mallorca with steps on the other side of the street. This way, an underpass was created which would be in semi-darkness.

Gaudí wanted to make the most of this lack of light in order to represent Hell. In this zone would appear demonic creatures, heresies, false gods, schisms, etc. Gaudí envisaged its style as oscillating between expressionism and popular art.

PROCESS
THE CONCEPTION OF THE BAPTISTERY

The Baptistery
By means of baptism, man purifies his sins and begins to form part of the Church and for this reason Gaudí gave the baptistery a pre-eminent position on the façade. It has three doors: one connects with the street, another with the cloister and the last one, with the temple.

Columns and doorways

Gaudí planned seven exterior columns to sustain the portico, on which are inscribed the seven gifts from the Holy Spirit. On the base of the columns are the Seven Deadly Sins and on the capitals their opposite virtues. Each one of the seven doors that lead into the temple is dedicated to a church sacrament and to a petition of the Lord's Prayer. All the doors have different depths due to the wall's undulating shape. The door that projects out the most will be the central one, which is subdivided into three doorways. The rest lead into the central lateral naves, two on each side, such as the Baptistery, situated on the left of the façade, and the Penitence chapel, situated on the right.

 1º

The Baptism door
Its petition is: "Our Father who art in heaven, hallowed be thy name".

 2º

The Extreme Unction door
Is the rite which is given to the dying: "Come to us your Kingdom".

 3º

The Order door
This entrance makes reference to the priesthood: "Thy will be done, on Earth as it is in Heaven".

 4º

The Eucharist door
Door which leads to the nave: "Give us today our daily bread".

 5º

The Confirmation door
"Forgive us our trespasses, as we forgive those who trespass against us".

 6º

The Matrimony door
The sacrament is matrimony and tells us: "Lead us not into temptation".

 **7º**

The Penitence door
Provides access to the Penitence chapel. It is related to: "Deliver us from evil".

 The construction of the Sagrada Familia is slow, because the Master of this work isn't in a hurry"

Antoni Gaudí

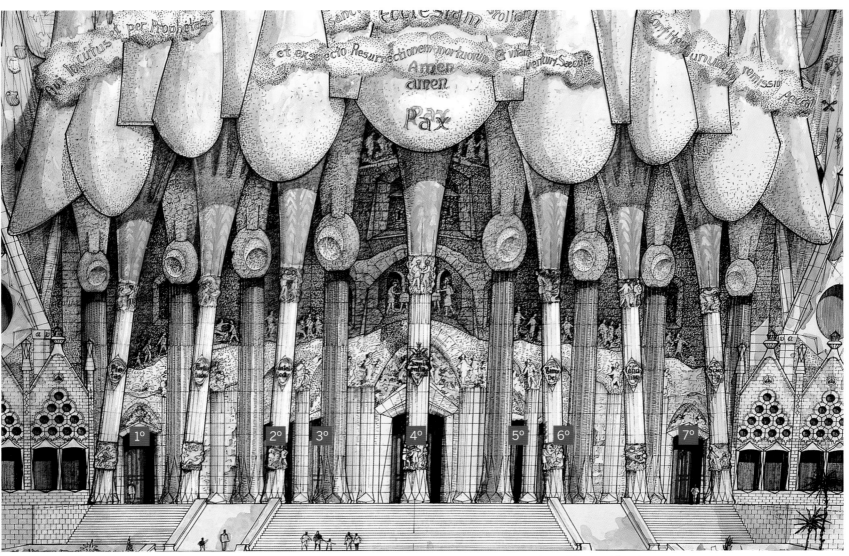

The Glory portico. In this drawing, carried out by Berenguer, one can appreciate the sheer dimensions of the steps, columns and doors of the temple's main entrance.

08

THE TEMPLE TOWERS

TOUCHING HEAVEN

By endowing the temple exterior with a great height Gaudí ensured that it would be the most striking construction in the city.

In any period or civilization, religious constructions have striven to differentiate themselves from other buildings by their shape and, above all, by their dimensions. Height bestows prestige and dignity upon a building that is itself a mystic symbol, representing the union of man with God. For this reason, Antoni Gaudí wanted his temple to be higher than any other building in Barcelona and its exterior was endowed with extraordinary dimensions. This monument is made up of eighteen towers whose heights are determined according to their religious hierarchy and the symbolic message that they represent. Therefore, the central cimborio, the highest and most important, is the one that represents Jesus Christ and measures 170 metres high and is crowned with a 15 metre high cross. Surrounding his cimborio are four towers dedicated to the four evangelists, measuring 125 metres high, while the cimborio that is devoted to the Virgin Mary reaches 120 metres and soars over the apse. Lastly, in order of height the twelve bell towers that represent the apostles serve as backdrop to the three façades. Their parabolic profile, like enormous needles piercing and cutting through the city skyline, make the bell towers the most characteristic element of the temple. When all of the towers are erected, the Sagrada Familia will majestically surpass any other Christian church built by Man.

THE TEMPLE TOWERS

Their enormous spires define Barcelona's panorama

The exterior of the monument holds an extraordinary symbolism, which Gaudí knew how to give expression to with four models of towers. The four rising from the three façades represent the twelve apostles. Over the temple is situated the highest tower, which symbolizes Jesus. This is surrounded by four cimborios which are dedicated to the evangelists. Lastly, the apse is covered by a large tower dedicated to Mary.

The lighthouse of Barcelona

Gaudí wanted the towers of Sagrada Familia to be higher than any other civil building in the city to demonstrate the supremacy of the divine over the human. The temple had to be the urban landscape's reference point and, therefore be visible from all corners of Barcelona. With this objective in mind, the central cimborio was planned, dedicated to Jesus, measuring 170 metres high, just a few metres less than that of the nearby mountain of Montjuïc. By way of surrendering to Nature, the architect upheld his belief that Man can't outdo what God has created.

View from the mountain
Owing to their great height, the towers of Sagrada Familia stand out from the rest of the buildings, their silhouette transforming them into the city's symbol.

1925

THE FIRST BELL TOWER IS FINISHED
The Saint Barnabus tower was the first one built and the only one finished in Gaudí's lifetime. The bell towers on this façade were completed in 1930.

COMPARISON
THE TEMPLE AND OTHER STRUCTURES

As work gathered momentum, the Sagrada Familia would unveil her real splendour. The central tower of the temple dedicated to Jesus, at 170 metres high soars higher than many of the most emblematic monuments of the world.

Pisa Tower **55 m**
St. Basil's Cathedral **60 m**
Statue of Liberty **93 m**
Big Ben **98 m**
Sagrada Familia **170 m**

1 **+100**
METRES
Apostle bell towers.

2 **120**
METRES
Virgin Mary tower.

3 **125**
METRES
The Evangelist towers.

4 **170**
METRES
Jesus' tower.

The inspiration

The originality of the work of Antoni Gaudí surged from his imagination, but also stemmed from his penetrating and analytical observation of reality. He himself recognised that a great part of his merit stemmed from his capacity to observe what tends to go unnoticed by others. The singular conical shape of the towers has been compared with three very different realities: the human towers made by the "castellers", the north African mosques and the geological formations in the Valley of the Fairies in Turkey.

The castellers. Gaudí confirmed that his towers obeyed the same law of equilibrium as the human towers or *castells*, a deep rooted tradition in Catalonia.

GLORY FAÇADE

PASSION FAÇADE

> " The shape of the towers, vertical and parabolic, is the union of gravity with light... in the upper part there will be luminous lights, like the natural light that comes from the sky"
>
> Antoni Gaudí

African Mosque
In 1892, Gaudí travelled to Tangiers to lead the project on the Franciscan Catholic missions and it was there that he discovered this original way of building.

The Valley of the Fairies, Turkey
Antoni Gaudí was also inspired by the curious and diverse geological formations of Capadocia, which is in the east of Turkey.

Apostle towers
Are different heights, from 100 to 118 metres.

The arrangement of the temple in 1910. The drawing of the exterior, done by Joan Rubió, one of the architects who assisted Antoni Gaudi, shows the sheer dimensions of the temple.

THE BELL TOWERS

Are located on the Nativity, Passion and Glory façades and represent the twelve apostles of Jesus.

The bell tower terminations

Gaudí thought of two complex solutions for the twelve bell tower endings. The first one consisted of a look-out tower with a hexagonal base and pyramidal shape with rings. The second proposal, which was the one chosen in the end and carried out, meant that each tower was topped with a pinnacle decorated with Venetian polychromatic mosaic work and crowned with a double-sided shield, a cross and white spheres, in reference to the Episcopal mitre.

The shield
The termination represents the two sides of the mitre. On one of the sides there is a golden cross and on the other appears the initial letter of the apostle to whom the temple is dedicated.

The hollow for the floodlights
This zone is planned for two lights: one is directed towards the street and the other, towards the central cimborios, to illuminate them at night.

Prayers
On each ending there are six vertical signs which alternately read *Hosanna* and *Excelsis*. Each letter is written in a hexagonal square.

Vents to direct the sound
Antoni Gaudí tilted the ledges of the windows in order that the sound of the bells would be heard throughout the city.

Construction of the bell towers. The first bell towers to be built were those of the Nativity façade. The only tower that Gaudí saw completed out of the four towers was the tower dedicated to Saint Barnabus, which was finished in 1925, a year before he died. Work on the towers of the Passion façade was finished in 1978.

The pinnacles

Measuring 25 metres high, the tower pinnacles stand out from the rest of the bell towers for their complex shape and rich coloured mosaic patterns they are covered with. This variety of shape, colour and material means, as well as a spectacular aesthetic effect, that the pinnacles are visible from far away. Gaudí used these decorative elements to unite the four symbols that represent bishops: the mitre, cross, staff and ring. The reason for which these Episcopal symbols are represented on the peak of the bell towers is that the bishops are responsible for carrying on the evangelical work of the first apostles.

The mitre
The mitre or head-dress worn by bishops is represented by the double-sided cross decorated with white balls.

The staff
The higher trunk of the pinnacle leans a little in its upper part to simulate the curved shape of the staff.

The ring
A symbol of authority, the Episcopal ring is below the pinnacle's trunk.

Pinnacle. The apostle Barnabus' initial.

DATA
THE PINNACLE GLASS

The Venetian glass
To decorate the pinnacles, Gaudí chose Venetian mosaic work, which is characterized by the fine quality glass which it is made from. It comes from Murano, an island world famous for its strong elegant glass, handcrafted since the 15th century.

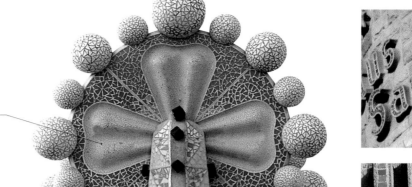

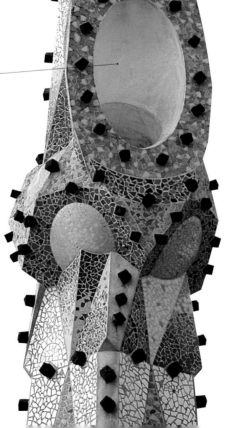

The phrases

On the bell towers, the word *Sanctus* is repeated and decorated in colour ceramic work. Each group of three *Sanctus* is dedicated to the Father, the Son and the Holy Spirit. Also carved in stone palm leaves are the names of the Holy Family and the expression *Sursum Corda* that in Latin stands for *lift up your hearts*.

INSIDE THE BELL TOWERS

Propelled by his non-conformist spirit, Gaudí carried out an acoustic study in order that the sound from the bells would be perfect as the rest of the temple.

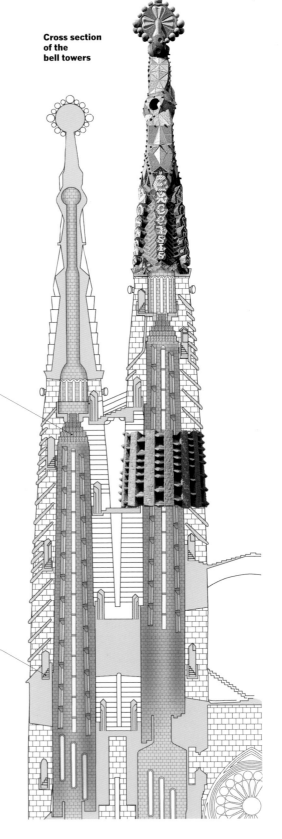

Cross section of the bell towers

* **The interior**
The stairs climb between the outer walls of the tower. The hollow inside is reserved for the bell.

Space for the bells
The temple will have 60 bells that will hang inside the bell towers, where they will obtain their optimum acoustic rendition.

The tubular bell
The tubular bells will be fixed and will be struck by hammers triggered by an electronic mechanism connected to a keyboard, as if it were an enormous piano which, moreover, will be able to reproduce any note.

Interior corridor
At a certain height in the bell towers, there is a corridor which the stairs pass through.

The base
The bell towers of the Nativity façade have a square base, but after 20 metres (approximately a fifth of their height), they become a circular shape.

The temple's voice

Gaudí wanted the bell towers to become the voice of the temple, which meant they had to have a rich finely tuned sound and be heard across the city. He therefore studied at length the quality of different types of bells. He finally decided that the temple would have three varieties: common ones, others tuned to the notes *mi, sol* and *do* and the tubular ones that he designed specially.

The walkways. The bell towers on this façade are connected by means of bridges and raised walkways.

The tubular bell

01

The winding staircase

The winding snail-shape stairs are situated in the lower part of the bell towers. Due to their narrowness, one has the sensation of going back on oneself. In order to create a much more interesting effect, Antoni Gaudí planned that in each pair of bell towers the stairs would turn in opposite directions. The winding staircases reach the height of the balconies and from then on, the stairs cling to the exterior walls, given that the hole in the centre of the tower is reserved for the bells.

426
STEPS

are in the towers. Climbing them requires a great physical effort but is more than compensated for by their magnificent views.

02

Nature

Gaudí managed to reproduce nature with surprising accuracy, as can be observed when comparing the staircase with that of a snail shell.

03

Interior corridor

The bell towers have interior stairs, which climb between the outer walls and the hollow reserved for the bells.

THE CIMBORIOS

The six central cimborios allowed the exterior of the temple to reach its maximum apogee. Jesus' cross and the evangelist sculptures, being the highest elements, symbolically dominate the entire monument.

Jesus' tower

The central cimborio represents Jesus and thus is the most monumental of all. From its top part the words *Amén* and *Aleluya* will descend, and as a symbol of the triumph of Christ it will be topped off by an enormous 4 armed cross which will reach 15 metres high. In its central part the cross will contain a lamb. The striking Venetian mosaics on its roof will make the cimborio gleam in the sunlight.

"This mosaic explosion is the first thing that sailors will see on approaching Barcelona. It will be a radiant welcome!"

Antoni Gaudí

The four-armed cross. The three-dimensional cross developed by Gaudí was repeatedly used in many of his works.

Park Güell

Bellesguard

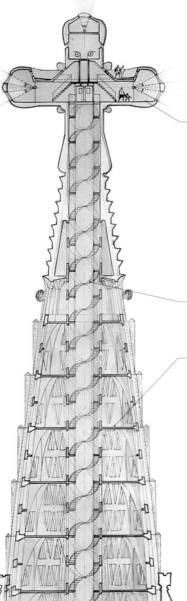

Cross section
Inside Jesus' tower.

Viewing platform
The cross will have a lookout point accessed by lift.

Night time illumination
From the four arms of the cross will shine four powerful beams of light which will be visible far away.

Stairs
Connects various floors in the tower.

Floors
The central cimborio is divided horizontally into thirteen floors.

✳ The cimborios
Of square or octagonal base, the cimborios are towers rising above the transept of a church or temple designed to illuminate the naves within. In the case of the Sagrada Familia, there are two of them.

Mary's tower

The cimborio dedicated to the Virgin Mary is on the apse side, following Byzantine tradition. The most spectacular element of this tower is the star crowning it.

It is a large shining star that represents the *Stella matutina* (the morning star), symbolizing that, just like this star announces dawn, Mary preceded the coming of Jesus.

View of Mary's cimborio vault

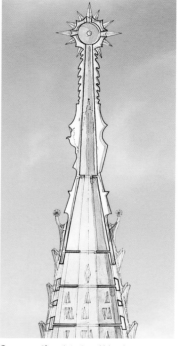

Cross section. Interior of Mary's tower.

PROCESS
CONSTRUCTION OF THE CIMBORIOS

The sacristy as an experiment for the cimborios
The six central towers have a structure which is similar to the sacristies, although on a larger scale. For this reason, Gaudí had foreseen that the construction of the sacristy would act as an experiment to define the shape and the details of the cimborios. This way, they could also study the possible problems that could come about when more height was added.

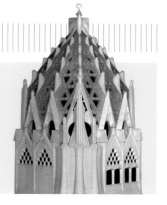

The highest towers of the temple

JESUS' TOWER

MARY'S TOWER

THE EVANGELIST TOWERS

The four cimborios dedicated to the evangelists surround the largest cimborio, dedicated to Jesus, reminding us that they were chosen to spread the word of Christ. Each cimborio will be crowned by a symbol that best represents its evangelist. At night, two lights will brightly beam from these towers: one will project towards the street (symbolizing the light from the Gospel illuminating the earthly world of man) and the other will illuminate the tower of Jesus, to remind humanity of his divinity.

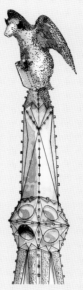

LUKE
Author of the third Gospel and symbolized by an ox. He was companion to Saint Peter.

MATTHEW
Was apostle to Jesus Christ and the author of the first Gospel. His traditional symbol is an angel.

MARK
Is the author of the second Gospel and is symbolized by a lion. He was Saint Peter's interpreter.

JOHN
Symbolized by the eagle, he was apostle to Jesus. He is the author of the fourth Gospel and the Apocalypse.

01
Bell towers
Close-up of one of the letters on the bell towers.

02
Star-like pinnacle
This pinnacle which is above the sculpture of the apostle Simon tops off the niches.

03
Bartholomew apostle
Passion façade.

04
The phrases
On the bell towers the words *Hosanna* and *Excelsis* can be read.

05
Bosses
Close-up of one of the 12 bosses that decorate each bell tower.

06
Bell tower of Philip the apostle
The balcony marks the transition from the tower's rhombus shaped floor to ellipse shaped floor.

07
Pinnacle detail
Because of its high quality, Gaudí decided to decorate the pinnacles with Venetian glass.

08
Pinnacle of the apostle Matthias
Of complex shape and lively colour, the pinnacles represent the bishops who continue with the apostles' mission.

A HARMONIOUS AND INNOVATIVE TEMPLE

The essence of Gaudí's architecture is concentrated within the Sagrada Familia: its column and vault system has no equivalent in the history of architecture.

The Latin cross ground plan is the only concession that Gaudí made to classical structures in the temple interior. The rest of the architectonic elements of which it is comprised are, as most of Gaudí's work, totally original. The solution for the temple naves was subject to an in-depth study and much consideration, which led to three different projects until a totally innovative architectonic solution was found. The first project, presented in 1898, was basically

Gothic, although the need for buttresses had been corrected. Due to a detailed study of weights, Gaudí managed to transfer pressure from the vaults directly to the floor by using extremely canted arches. Nevertheless, this project didn't fully satisfy the architect for two reasons: the temple continued being, in essence, Gothic and each arch mechanically depended on the adjoining one, so if one failed, it would drag the other one down in its fall. It was then at the age of 70 that Gaudí

found the solution he so yearned for, in the use of arboreal columns. These columns, tilting and branching out like a tree, meant buttresses could be avoided, as the weight of the roof would be directed to the floor thus freeing the outer walls. This ingenious architectural system has, likewise, a spectacular aesthetic consequence, as the temple interior is transformed into an enormous stone forest, where light harmoniously filters through its vaults and outer walls.

THE TEMPLE INTERIOR
Antoni Gaudí imagined it as a colossal mystic forest

Just like on the temple exterior, Gaudí bestowed a symbolic value on each element inside the temple. The whole monument is an exaltation of the Faith and represents the universal Church. With its tree-like columns, Gaudí wanted the Sagrada Familia to be an enormous spiritual forest, a place of prayer, where the believer feels protected and united with God.

The symbolic dimensions
Inside the temple the four daily prayers are represented, just like the Gospels and epistles that are read out in Sunday mass. To illuminate the area where liturgy takes place, there will be a lamp with seven arms symbolizing the Holy Spirit. As in all Christian temples, the main altar will be presided over by a cross, from which will surge a vine whose tendrils and grapes will form the baldachin that covers it. To complete the Holy Trinity, the apse tower will be covered with mosaic work and the vestments of God will be symbolized on its celestial vault.

The interior
Berenguer's illustration shows the central altar area. This altar will be positioned below a triumphant arch from which a baldachin will hang.

Rose windows
Made during the first years of construction on the temple they recall the style of Gothic cathedrals.

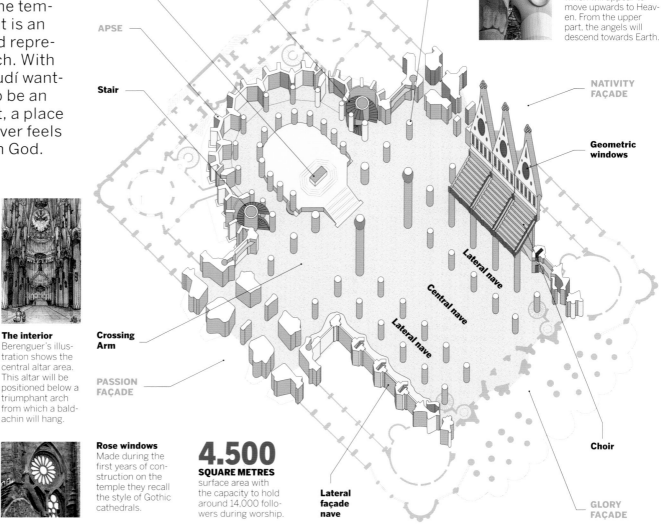

Altar

Stair

APSE

Stair

Crossing Arm

PASSION FAÇADE

Arboreal columns
Each column will carry the image of a saint which will appear to move upwards to Heaven. From the upper part, the angels will descend towards Earth.

NATIVITY FAÇADE

Geometric windows

Lateral nave

Central nave

Lateral nave

Choir

Lateral façade nave

GLORY FAÇADE

4.500 SQUARE METRES
surface area with the capacity to hold around 14,000 followers during worship.

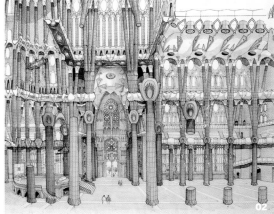

01

3D view
Three-dimensional drawing done on computer of the central nave and apse interior.

02

Drawing of the interior
This illustration by Berenguer shows the doorway of the Nativity façade. On the left the altar can be seen.

03

Catalan vault
Is used on all of the central nave.

04

Nativity façade interior
Built between 1894 and 1930, the façade interior has a large quantity of uncarved stones. Gaudí said that once the temple was covered and protected from the sun and rain, the sculptor would be able to work better.

THE FIVE NAVES

In search of the perfect temple, Gaudí paid special attention to the symbolic and spiritual importance of the interior, by creating an innovative architectural style whilst endowing it with monumental dimensions.

A temple of huge dimensions

The temple has a Latin cross ground plan and is made up of five longitudinal naves, with a transept measuring 60 metres long by 45 metres wide. The total length, from the entrance to the apse, is 90 metres. The central nave is 15 metres wide with the lateral ones measuring half : 7.5m. The central nave vaults reach a height of 45 metres, while the lateral nave ones reach 30 metres. The vaults situated below the central cimborio reach 60 metres and those of the apse soar to 75. With these dimensions, the Sagrada Familia will be one of the largest temples in the world.

1.200
PEOPLE SINGING
make up the adult chorus. The child choir will be made up of 350 children.

30
METRES
is the height reached by the vaults of the four lateral naves.

45
METRES
is the height of the central nave.

Window
To illuminate the temple, Gaudí included numerous windows.

The Choir
Located on the lateral naves is the gallery for the adult choir, who will sing in big celebrations. The choir gallery is focused towards the large altar and is accessed by means of a winding staircase. The child choir will be located on the apse side and be comprised of 350 children.

> **The temple interior will be like a forest"**
> Antoni Gaudí

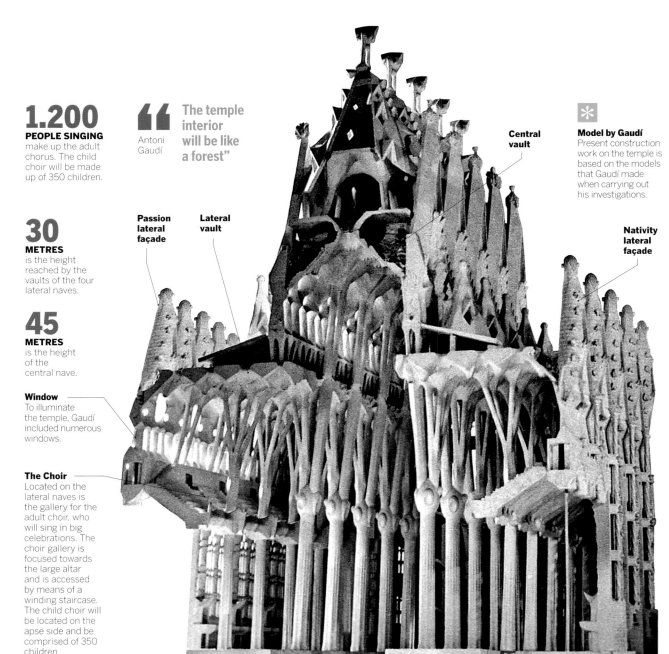

Passion lateral façade

Lateral vault

Central vault

Model by Gaudí
Present construction work on the temple is based on the models that Gaudí made when carrying out his investigations.

Nativity lateral façade

Original model by Gaudí, 1921-1926

1987 Work commences on the foundations of the columns and windows.

1989 Various columns and lateral windows have been erected.

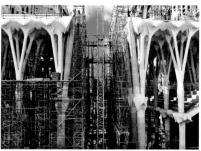

1997 On completion of the lateral vaults, work on the central one commences.

1999 The central vaults are finished and those of the transept are planned.

* The walls
As the nave lateral walls only support their own weight, it is possible to put in many large windows, which allow a better illumination of the temple.

Phrases
On the exterior of the temple, between the windows are written allegorical legends such as *oració* (prayer), *thus* (incense) and *aurum* (gold).

The nave lateral façades

Thanks to the ingenious arboreal system that Gaudí used in the temple interior, the lateral walls are freed from supporting the roof weight. In contrast to other styles, like the Romanic or Gothic styles, Gaudí's lateral façades only have to support their own structure, meaning they can be much lighter. One of the main consequences of this greater lightness is that it provides more liberty when opening up spaces for the entrance of natural light. Therefore, all the walls are dotted with numerous windows of various shape and size by which the temple's naves are harmoniously illuminated.

The fruit on the exterior

Carried out by Japanese sculptor Etsuro Sotoo, the apexes on the exterior walls bestow on the temple a naturalist air. Crowned with baskets, such as figs and apples, these elements symbolize the fruit that the Holy Spirit scattered on Earth.

 The fruit
Positioned on the endings of the lateral façades, the baskets of fruit are represented by coloured spheres, finely covered with polychromatic mosaic.

The founding saints
On the exterior, on the upper part between the windows are the statues of founding saints of religious orders. There are ten in total.

Saint Joaquina of Vedruna

Saint Juan Bosco

Saint José Oriol

01

Grapes and wine

The terminations of the various pinnacles of the central nave, carried out by Etsuro Sotoo, are used to exhibit the grapes and wine as symbol of the Eucharist. There are also endings that represent the wheat of bread.

02

The fruit

The sculptor Etsuro Sotoo also did the endings on the lateral façade pinnacles, which consist of baskets of fruit: apples, figs, peaches, loquats, pomegranates and cherries.

01

THE COLUMNS AND VAULTS

With the arboreal column, Gaudí found the mechanical solution and aesthetic spirit he sought for his temple. The arboreal structure culminated in vaults shaped like palm leaves.

The new column

Gaudí investigated for many years until he discovered a column that would mean he could avoid the use of buttresses. One of his innovations consisted in slightly tilting the columns in order to capture the weight of the roof in the most optimum way. Likewise, he turned the shaft in two directions to achieve greater resistance and a spectacular aesthetic effect.

The arboreal column

During many years of study, Gaudí wanted the temple columns to be as robust and beautiful as the trees in a forest. The architect fled from vertical rigidity by tilting and turning them in spiral form to simulate how a tree trunk grows. Likewise, when they reached a certain height, the columns divided out into branchlike form to increase the number of support elements and to better distribute the weight of the roofs and the vaults. This arboreal design allowed Gaudí to optimise the different loads and to be able to lessen the diameter of all the columns.

A first study. Gaudí experimented with tilting and helicoid columns in Park Güell and various other works.

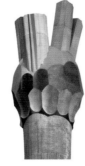

The nodes

The nodes are the elements of transition between columns. Gaudí used them to mark the point where the columns branch out.

The roofs

The central nave's ceiling is comprised of a series of pyramids, each one crowned with a lantern and light, reaching 70 metres high. Built with Montjuïc stone, they will be decorated with shields, similar to those on the bell towers and will have the inscription *amen* and *al-le-lu-ia*.

Central nave roof
This model, an Antoni Gaudí original, was the definitive solution for the temple roof.

Computer simulation
In the current construction work the original models are combined with the latest technology.

Study model
Vault and arboreal column on the lateral nave, a Gaudí original (1920-1926).

Azimuthal view of the vaults
The star-like vaults have orifices through which light enters.

1924
THE DEFINITIVE SOLUTION
Gaudí abandoned the idea of the ribbed vault system for the hyperbolic vault system.

The vaults

In contrast to former cathedrals, whose vaults were robust and had to support a lot of weight, Gaudí wanted Sagrada Familia's vaults to be light-weight and illuminate the temple interior. The vaults emerge from tree-like columns and form palm leaves which represent the symbol of martyrdom. The assembly point of the leaves, some concave and others convex, also allow the filtering of light into the temple.

Vault location. The vaults covering the temple are at the same time protected by the general roof.

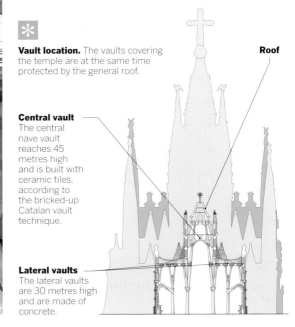

Roof

Central vault
The central nave vault reaches 45 metres high and is built with ceramic tiles, according to the bricked-up Catalan vault technique.

Lateral vaults
The lateral vaults are 30 metres high and are made of concrete.

THE ILLUMINATION AND THE WINDOWS

Thanks to the architectonic advantages that the arboreal column offered, Gaudí managed to provide the interior with a uniform light in keeping with the spiritual aestheticism he sought for the temple.

The temple of light

The windows, the vaults and, in general, all the sources of light were designed to illuminate the temple interior the same way as light filters through the leaves in a forest. Gaudí pursued a harmonious indirect illumination, which highlighted the plasticity of the architecture, while at the same time showed off the temple's decoration and transmitted a feeling of spiritual peace.

The diffusers
Created by Gaudí, they are fitted into the holes in the vaults. They are a type of lamp made of metal mesh to diffuse the sunlight. They also use electric light to light up the temple at night.

Natural light
Sun light will illuminate the temple in a gentle and harmonious manner thanks to the curious shape and arrangement of the vaults, which act as luminance diffusers, and by the windows which go round the temple.

Electrical lighting
The lamps are placed and designed so that they illuminate just like natural light does.

The evolution of the windows

In consonance with their creator's artistic search, the windows experience a clear evolution from the neo-gothic style of the crypt to the reinterpretation of the Gothic that Gaudí made in those of the central nave.

1 Gothic
In the lower windows, although possessing new shapes, the Gothic structure is retained, with its honeycomb shape and large circular rose window.

2 Geometric
The evolution towards a honeycomb shape gives way to new geometric forms, with a triangular fronton topping the window.

3 Geometric naturalism
The last window clearly shows the leap towards abstraction, in such a way that the number of elements is greatly simplified.

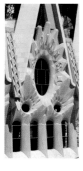

Joan Vila-Grau
The Catalan artist has been working on the stained glass windows of the temple since 1999, interpreting in his own way the chromatic concept devised by Gaudí. Thus, the lower windows will be of an intense colour, the higher ones of a lighter colour, whilst the windows of the central nave on the upper floor will be done in a combination of colourless glass of varying texture, which will illuminate the vaults better.

02 **03**

I am the light
The stained glass of the temple tracery, on which the phrase from the Gospel "I am the light" is symbolized. The stained glass windows are executed using the traditional technique of inserting coloured glass panes into a network of lead rods.

04

Rose window
Window on Nativity façade.

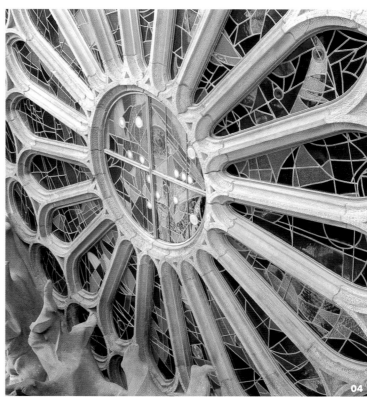

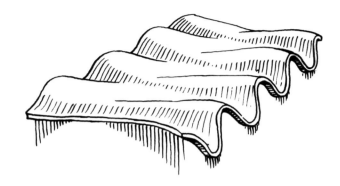

10

THE SCHOOLROOMS

THE GENIUS OF SIMPLICITY

The schoolrooms are a magnificent example of Gaudí's capacity to transform a humble material into a construction that is as surprising as it is technically impeccable.

Despite its small dimensions, the building that housed the provisional schoolrooms is considered as one of the most representative of Gaudí's works, given that simplicity, functionality and innovation are combined within. The Association of Devotees to Saint Joseph, promoters of the temple, along with the Father Gil Parés, chaplain of Sagrada Familia, paid great importance to primary and secondary education. For this reason it was Gil Parés who commissioned Gaudí to construct a small building that would serve as an educational centre for the children of the workers participating in the construction on the temple and for the children in the neighbourhood. The architect responded by constructing an extremely economical and practical building. Built with Catalan brick, which wasn't rendered over, Gaudí divided the interior of the building by means of two walls, giving rise to three classrooms. Moreover, the architect used three metallic pillars to support the master beam on which the roof beams rested. Undoubtedly, the structure's conodial cover is the most surprising and distinctive element of the building. The innovative spirit of the work perfectly identified with the pedagogical system used in education. The religious Gil Parés' views on education were very progressive for the period as he believed in the active school, where practical and instructive knowledge prevailed. The schoolrooms were in use from 1909 until the late eighties, when the lack of students led to its closure as educational centre.

THE SCHOOLROOMS
One of the most simple and ingenious buildings by Gaudí

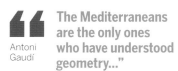
In a corner of the grounds of Sagrada Familia there is a building of apparent modesty and small dimensions. *Las Escuelas* (the schoolrooms), which Gaudí designed, were built for the children of the workmen and families of the neighbourhood. The simplicity of this construction is deceptive, given that, as with all of Gaudí's work, its exterior reflects the aesthetic originality of its creator and its structure, his innovative technical solutions.

Simple and rational

The schoolrooms were built between 1908 and 1909 and functioned as a teaching centre for more than 70 years. Their external appearance is of great simplicity as they would be demolished as soon as more space was needed in the temple grounds and Gaudí also wanted minimal cost. The most distinctive feature of the building is its undulating roof and walls. The sinuous form provides the structure with a great resistance in a simple and rational way. For example, the walls offer an appearance of great rigidity, in spite of being built with two layers of vertically positioned brick.

Education
In the schoolrooms a method known as "active pedagogy" was followed. Its objective was that education was practical and that the student would get involved.

9.000
PESETAS
was how much it cost to build the schoolrooms. It is believed that Gaudí paid the 9000 pesetas from his own pocket (around 54 euros.)

The fire of 1936

In July 1936, shortly after the start of the Spanish Civil War, an uncontrolled group of people set fire to the schoolrooms. The fire badly affected the building and its roof collapsed. The architect F. Quintana took charge of its reconstruction introducing various modifications to Gaudí's building.

1936
THE SCHOOLROOMS
catch fire along with other parts of the Sagrada Familia, at the start of the Civil War.

Destruction
This serious fire provoked the collapse of the roof.

The ground plan
The interior has three school-rooms, which can hold up to 150 pupils. Placed on either end of the building are the toilets, which are accessed from the classroom or playground.

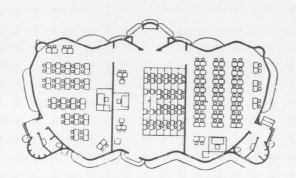

Studies done by Le Corbusier in 1928
Considered as father of modern architecture, Swiss architect Le Corbusier marvelled at Gaudí's schoolrooms when visiting the temple in 1928.

Materials and dimensions
Built with brick, one of Gaudí's preferred materials. Its maximum height reaches six metres and its base occupies a space of 24x12 metres.

The roof
The roof's undulations allow the water to pour out on either side in an original and practical way.

Brickwork
The characteristics of this kind of brick mean that any type of surface can be generated.

Twisting surfaces
In spite of their apparent thinness, the roof and the walls have a great structural resistance generated by their undulating shape.

Entrance
View of a door which provides access to the construction's interior.

Windows
It boasts 19 windows distributed along the length of the perimeter.

Drawings generated by computer
The school's roof and wall undulations, where the uneven height of the walls can be seen.

A NEW USE FOR THE SCHOOLROOMS

By moving the schoolrooms, work on the temple could continue. This change was also used as an opportunity to recuperate their original appearance and replace the original materials lost during their reconstruction in 1936.

The schoolrooms change location

The need to change the position of the schools couldn't be put off any more as their location prevented work progressing on the temple. In order that the transferred building was as faithful as possible to the original, Gaudí's construction method was studied and a copy was even built in the locality of Badalona. The elements that were preserved the best were translated whole and each piece was put into its respective place, integrating the recovered materials with the new ones.

The pieces
A large part of the original building was moved by being cut up into parts. For the move, each one of these pieces was reinforced with a metallic structure and a crane would then put the parts in the right place.

14
TONNES
was how much the pieces of the original building weighed.

The move and reconstruction
The new parts of the building have been constructed according to the technique used in Gaudí's time.

Step by step

Firstly, the foundations and the base structure were laid. Next, the parts that were in the best condition were moved in their entirety, such as the frontons, then the rest of the structural elements were integrated. The roof was the last thing to be built.

01. The walls were raised and the original pieces put into place.

02. The iron master beam was positioned and the wooden beams.

03. The ceiling was built using three layers of brick.

PROCESS
EVOLUTION OF THE SCHOOLS

The transfer would mean the large-scale retrieval of the original spirit of the schoolrooms. The only new contribution added to the new building was the thermal insulation of the roof.

1909
2002

The interior
The museum possesses didactic material that explains the geometry that Gaudí used to build the temple.

1994
THIS YEAR
the necessity arises to transfer the schoolrooms so that the temple's lateral nave could be built.

2002
WAS THE YEAR
that the schools were moved and the working museum of Gaudí was inaugurated.

Gaudí's workshop

At present, the schoolrooms house the didactic room of the Sagrada Familia museum. Amongst other curiosities, there is a replica of Gaudí's work table, given that the original was in his studio near the apse, and the work table is where he would lay out his plans and plaster cast models. Models of the Glory façade, the sacristies and the columns can also be viewed. By means of abundant academic material, Gaudí's principal technical innovations and the basis for his revolutionary architecture are explained in detail here. There is also an area dedicated to the history of the schoolrooms.

Gaudí's geometric elements
The architect had a diversity of slides, which he used to study the twisting surfaces.

Funicular model
With this type of model, Gaudí studied the structure's arches and its respective loads.

The museum has a replica of Gaudí's work table

Sacristy model made in plaster
The museum has various plaster models and plans, which are original to Antoni Gaudí.

01

The class
One of the move's objectives was to recuperate the original appearance of Gaudí's building, lost after its reconstruction in 1936.

02

Accessory
A fake bell is next to one of the entrance doors.

03

Lamps
The room preserves period lighting.

04

Undulating roof
The sinuous shape fortifies the construction in a simple and rational way.

05

Windows
Planned to be demolished as work progressed, the windows are of great simplicity.

06

Rainfall drainage
The endings of the undulating roof also function as a means of draining away rain water.

07

The schoolrooms towards 1920
The original position of the building was on Mallorca Street.

TEMPLE OF THE SAGRADA FAMILIA,
THE MASTERPIECE OF ANTONI GAUDÍ

© PUBLISHED BY
2006, MUNDO FLIP EDICIONES, S.C.P.

TEXTS
MANAGING DIRECTORS: CARLOS GIORDANO Y NICOLÁS PALMISANO
REDACTION: MARÍA JOSÉ GÓMEZ GIMENO
TRANSLATIONS: CERYS R. JONES
© CARLOS GIORDANO Y NICOLÁS PALMISANO

PHOTOGRAPHS
CARLOS GIORDANO & NICOLÁS PALMISANO

© PHOTOGRAPHS OF TEMPLE INTERIOR AND MUSEUM
CARLOS GIORDANO, NICOLÁS PALMISANO &
JUNTA CONSTRUCTORA DEL TEMPLE EXPIATORI
DE LA SAGRADA FAMÍLIA

© ARCHIVE PHOTOGRAPHS
JUNTA CONSTRUCTORA DEL TEMPLE EXPIATORI
DE LA SAGRADA FAMÍLIA

© ILLUSTRATIONS AND PLANS
CARLOS GIORDANO & NICOLÁS PALMISANO
(PAGES: 21, 23, 24, 25, 32, 35, 44, 45, 47, 109, 110, 114, 122, 129, 137)

© ARCHITECTONIC WORK
JUNTA CONSTRUCTORA DEL TEMPLE EXPIATORI
DE LA SAGRADA FAMÍLIA

FIRST EDITION, 2006

ISBN
84-934492-5-3

DEPÓSITO LEGAL
B-13876-2006

PRINTED IN SPAIN
I.G. MARMOL S.L.

MUNDO FLIP EDICIONES
www.mundoflip.com :: info@mundoflip.com

Temple Expiatori de la
SAGRADA FAMÍLIA

WITH THE
COLLABORATION OF THE
JUNTA CONSTRUCTORA
DEL TEMPLE EXPIATORI
DE LA SAGRADA FAMILIA